WHEN CHRISTIANS QUARREL

Jerry L. Schmalenberger, D. Min.

WHEN CHRISTIANS QUARREL

ISBN 0-89536-276-7

PRINTED IN U.S.A.

In memory of my father,
from whom I learned faithfulness,
and to mother,
who lives it.

CONTENTS

Fifteenth Sunday after Pentecost
Matthew 16:21-26

Cross-Bearing

The time was close to the time when Jesus was crucified. The Scripture tells us that Jesus had just told the disciples that he was going to have to suffer and be put to death. Peter couldn't stand that idea and told him, "This shall never happen to you." (Matthew 16:22b) Jesus told Peter that he was thinking the way people thought rather than the way God thought. Then Jesus told his disciples what the Christian life was all about. It is one of the recurring themes of Jesus' teaching. He said these things over and over again. We find them in Matthew 10:34, Mark 8:34, Luke 9:23, and John 12:25.

He said if we really wanted to be his disciples, this is what we would have to do: "If anyone wants to come with me, he must forget himself, carry his cross, and follow me." (Matthew 16:24)

So today in our Scripture we have a challenge issued to us if we are really going to be with the Savior. Three things are required: 1. We must forget ourselves; 2. We must carry our cross; 3. We must follow Jesus.

Let's consider them one by one that our lives might also be a discipleship.

We must forget ourselves. The King James Bible puts it: ". . .deny himself." What Jesus is asking of us is that we put God first in all our considerations, that we remove ourselves from center stage and put God there. We wipe ourselves out as the top priority of life and put God as the ruling principle, the ruling passion of our life.

Zinzendorf asked John Wesley, "Do you think it was self-denial for the Lord Jesus to come down from heaven to rescue a world? Was it self-denial? No, it was love — love that swallows up everything, and first of all self."

During Lent, we talk a lot about self-denial. We usually think of that meaning to give up things and say "no" to certain habits or pleasures in our lives and use the money saved to contribute to the work of God's kingdom. While that is an admirable thing to do, and good discipline for our Christian lives, that's a small part of what it means when we say "forget one's self" or "deny one's self."

We live in an age when a lot of emphasis is put on our rights, our being comfortable, our getting what we deserve. Jesus is saying here that true discipleship involves a higher loyalty — a greater motivation than "getting ours." It means pouring ourselves into the cause of Christ and his church. It means putting God first above everything else.

In his book *Man the Unknown*, Alexis Carrel wrote, "While surrounded by comfort, beauty, and mechanical marvels, man fails to realize that he is degenerating." Then he adds, "Deny yourself, for there is no more beautiful adventure than the renovation and remaking of mankind."

How much happier our marriages could be; how much fuller our lives can be; how much better the stewardship of the church ought to be if we Christians were willing to follow this great challenge. There is a new and beautfiul way of life held out to us in this Scripture. To get ourselves off our own hands and concentrate on God is what we are asked to do. What a magnificent, joyful, abundant life we can live! Jesus says, "If anyone wants to come with me, he must forget himself." Then he adds, " . . . carry his cross . . ." And that's the second admonition to the Christian.

We must carry our cross. Here is the call to sacrifice in our lives. This is an element we don't talk about very much in our church anymore. Yet, the New Testament is full of the idea.

J. W. Hauley in *These Prophetic Voices* writes, "In old Russia when a commander wished to inspire a recruit with a challenge for service, he told of the sacrifice of Turkestan. The Russian army was small. The Asiatic foe came swooping down in overwhelming numbers. The guns had been halted a mile in the rear. Between the little army and the artillery lay a deep ditch which could not be crossed. It was guns now or annihilation. Immediately a whole company of infantry threw itself into the ditch and filled it to the brim with living bodies. The guns went over at a gallop, and the sacrifice of a company in the ditch saved not only an army, but a nation."

Our own comforts, our own pleasure, our own safety and rest and ease must from time to time be abandoned, and serving Christ and his cause has to come first. Our desire to sleep in a little later on Sunday must be put aside so that Church School classes are taught. Our desire to have beer in the refrigerator and seventy-two degrees temperature in our home may have to give way so that others can have milk for the baby and school rooms heated. We need the self-discipline of sacrifice; that is, cross-bearing to give our Christian life deeper significance.

Some time ago *Life* magazine printed a full-page picture entitled "Canned Pig." The pig entered the milk can to lap up some milk and got so bloated that it was unable to back out. The owner saved both pig and can by doing nothing. After eight hours of enforced dieting, the animal shrank down to normal size and got out by itself. Mark Twain used to tell of a Mississippi steamboat with a whistle so big that when they blew it, it took so much of the engine's steam that the boat dropped backwards. The self-seeking life is the self-defeating life, and though the fasting and prayer of Christian life are aimed at others, they also represent the only avenue to spiritual freedom and continuing growth.

Luke adds one word to this command that is not in Matthew's Gospel, "Let him take up his cross *daily.*" The very important element of cross-bearing and sacrifice is not one or two dramatic sacrifices in our own life, but rather a whole life-style which considers first the demands of God and needs of others. So much of the church's appeal is for coins and used clothing instead of providing an opportunity to really adopt a life-style — a way of life — which bears the cross, which calls for sacrifice on our part. The Christian life is a life which is always concerned with others more than itself.

It is not hard to understand the mood of Henry Watson Fowler, when at the age of forty-one he retired from his position as a school-teacher and said, "I'm never going to do a useful thing again." Sooner or later, everybody gets tired of duty, weary of responsibility, fed up with being helpful; but to eat the fruits of Christian faith and never plant the trees is both to be a parasite upon the past and to steal our own comfort from the pain of our own fellows.

There isn't a choice, really, if we are Christ's people, whether we pledge or tithe, or serve on a committee, or give our time and talent for Christ. Christ's people are "cross-bearers" and these opportunities to bear the cross we take immediately and do, and do with joy for the opportunity.

Any worthy person wants to pull his own weight in the boat. Any worthy person wants to carry his own share of the burden. And when the struggle is as crucial as the one we face today, and when every person worth his salt is exerting his utmost effort to push the Christian cause to victory, then the malingerers and loafers must stand the awful scrutiny of words like those of King Henry's sent to Crillon, "Hang yourself, brave Crillon; we have fought at Arques and you were not there."

Jesus said, "If anyone wants to come with me, he must forget himself, carry his cross, and follow me."

This is the third admonition: We must follow Jesus. To follow him is to be obedient to him. Follow-the-leader is a game that everyone knows. Remember how one person would lead out and the rest would try to mimic or do the exact same thing as the leader? I still see them do it on the ski slope, as the first person off the chair lift leads down the hill and the rest try to follow in the exact same tracks and perform the same maneuvers. I've seen it in the summer when a bunch of kids line up and go off the diving board at a swimming pool in the exact same fashion. Everything the leader does, you do, no matter how difficult or silly it may look. That's a good game. There is that element in following Jesus as our leader. The Christian life is a continual following, mimicking, doing as he did, obeying, in everything we do. We copy him in loving our enemy, submitting our lives to God, standing up for social justice, suffering hurt and embarrassment, being the salt and the leaven and the comfort of life.

He is sitting on a powder keg whose fuse has been lighted. He is draining the blood of the men who bear the burdens for him. It is inescapably hard to follow Jesus, but sooner or later we shall find that, in a world like our own, it is even harder not to follow him.

Those are the ways that Jesus says we are to live in our Christian life — by following him, by carrying the cross, and by forgetting ourselves.

Then Jesus adds — if we do this, then here is the result — verse 25 — "For whoever wants to save his own life will lose it, but whoever loses his life for my sake will find it." When we live life this way, we find real life. When we go at our Christianity with abandonment, we discover a bonus not expected!

So we have here the recipe for life as compared with existence. It's one thing to have a heartbeat and breath in our lungs — it's quite another to be alive. Playing it too safe stagnates our lives. But to throw ourselves into the cause of Christ with a certain recklessness, is to become alive and thrill to it.

In our day and generation, it is not the question of martyrdom as it was for those early Christians; but it is still true that if we run our lives safely, securely, with comfort and ease as a top priority, we are losing a lot that makes life for a Christian fullfilling and exciting.

Henry Knox Sherril IV wrote, "The joyful news that he is risen does not change the contemporary world. Still before us lie work, discipline, sacrifice. But the fact of Easter gives us the spiritual power to do the work and accept the discipline, and make the sacrifice."

George Bernard Shaw has said: "I am convinced that my life belongs to the whole community; and as long as I live, it is my privilege to do for it whatever I can, for the harder I work, the more I live. I rejoice in life for its own sake. Life is no brief candle for me. It is the sort of splendid torch which I got hold of for a Moment, and I want to make it burn as brightly as possible before turning it over to future generations."*

Our lives become soft and flabby, when they could be an adventure. We become earth-bound when we could be reaching for the stars. Let's be challenged and invited today by this Scripture: "Then Jesus said to his disciples, 'If anyone wants to come with me, he must forget himself, carry his cross, and follow me. For whoever wants to save his own life will lose it; but whoever loses his life for my own sake will find it.'" (Matthew 16:24-25.)

*A Treasury of Sermon Illustrations, by Charles L. Wallis, Abindgon Press.

Sixteenth Sunday after Pentecost
Matthew 18:15-20

When Christians Quarrel: Resolving Conflict in the Church

One of the things I like best about the New Testament is that it is so practical. It must have been the fact that Jesus had human beings called disciples always with him that forced him to speak in such everyday terms about everyday problems. Sometimes Christians disagree in the congregation of believers. Sometimes they quarrel. Sometimes they hold grudges against each other. The Scripture for today says that we must never tolerate any situation in which there is a breach of personal relationship between us and another member of the Christian community.

In this eighteenth chapter of Matthew Jesus admits that disciples are going to have conflicts; but they are to resolve them.

It is very true today that the behavior of us church members on this very issue makes Christianity to the outside world either repulsive or attractive.

It isn't a matter that Christians are perfect and will not have conflicts. There will always be quarrels, differences of opinion on how and who, disappointments with preachers and councils, hurt feelings, bent pride, loss of face, and lots of mistakes. It's the idea that Christians can resolve these conflicts as no other fellowship can, that Jesus puts before us today.

Comus, a Duke of Florence, had a saying that indicated the limitations of his religion: "You shall read that we are commanded to forgive our enemies, but you never read that we are commanded to forgive our friends."

That can happen in the Christian proclamation of the gospel. We spend a lot of time in our pulpits talking about how Christians are admonished by Jesus Christ to love their enemies and to pray for their enemies. When in actuality, right there in the pew side by side are Christians who hold grudges, hang on to petty hurts, refuse to forgive and love each other within the fellowship. And when they do this, church and Christianity and the whole practice of religion for them is not the joyful experience it ought to be. They miss a large dimension of belonging to God's family.

This particular portion of Matthew (18:15-18) gives us a whole scheme of action for the mending of broken relationships within our "family of God" called the Christian fellowship: Jesus advises, "If your brother sins against you, go and tell him his fault, between you and him alone."

I. The first rule Jesus gives us is that if anyone has wronged us, we should immediately put our complaint into words. One of the biggest mistakes we can make is not to voice our hurt. To just brood about it can be fatal. That can poison our whole life until we can't think of anything else but our own hurt. Our own personal injury becomes the whole center of our life.

A lot of times, just voicing such a hurt can help, and Jesus knew that. He said, ". . . go and tell him . . ." Many times just putting our disgruntlement into words will help us put it into its proper perspective. It may even seem trivial and a lot less important when we do this. There are so many times when we just must not suffer our hurt in a sort of brooding silence. That's the worst thing we can do. The first rule that Jesus gives us to resolve conflict is: tell it, speak it, get it out into the open.

Irving Stone, in *Love is Eternal*, concludes his narrative account of Mary Todd and Abraham Lincoln with an interview between Mrs. Lincoln and Parker, the President's guard: "Parker entered, a heavy-faced man with half-closed lips. He trembled. 'Why were you not at the door to keep the assassin out?' she asked fiercely. Parker hung his head. 'I have bitterly repented it. But I did not believe that anyone would try to kill so good a man in such a public place. The belief made me careless. I was attracted by the play. I did not see the assassin enter the box.' 'You should have seen him. You had no business to be careless.' She fell back on the pillow, covered her face with her hands. 'Go now. It's not you I can't forgive, it's the assassin.' 'If Pa had lived,' said Tad, 'he would have forgiven the man who shot him. Pa forgave everyone.'"

II. Second, we are advised to see the person in person. Jesus says ". . . go and tell him his fault, between you and him alone." (Matthew 18:15) And then he adds the beautiful thought, "If he listens to you, you have gained your brother."

If we have a difference with someone, Jesus says to settle it face to face. It seems to me that Jesus is warning against writing letters, complaining to someone else, and all such things. To write a letter can bring on more misunderstanding, while Christians can deal with each other face to face.

Humans who are in Christ can deal with each other differently. Being aware of our own shortcomings and still having God's forgiveness, we can deal with each other in a compassionate way allowing forgiveness. Knowing we also make mistakes, we can allow others the same privilege.

Emery Parks tells: "When the books of a certain Scotch doctor were examined after his death, it was found that a number of accounts were crossed out with a note: 'Forgiven — too poor to pay.' But the physician's wife decided that these accounts must be paid, and proceeded to sue for the money. The judge asked one question: 'Is this your husband's handwriting?' When she replied that it was, he said: 'Then there is no tribunal in the land that can obtain this money when he has written the word Forgiven."

Jesus says to go personally — a letter can be misread and misunderstood, and it can convey a tone which it never meant to convey. Jesus adds this, "If he listens to you, you have gained your brother." That's a beautiful picture! We make the effort — take the first step — go in Christian love — and there is a bonus in it for us! We have a brother or sister! Those with whom we have struggled and resolved conflict become the most precious of all to us.

Our purpose is not to humiliate or condemn, but to gain a brother or sister — to gain him or her for friendship and for the church of Christ.

Roy A. Burkhart told this story. Once a boy went out of his home to do something that his parents felt was wrong. He was involved in an accident and lost both legs. It was a terrible blow, but the father told me one of the most beautiful stories I have ever heard. He said, "When his mother and I saw him in the hospital cot lying there aware that he had lost both legs, he said, 'Will you forgive me?' They both ran up and hugged him and said, 'Of course; we have already forgiven you.' And he answered, 'Then I can live without my legs.' "

The first step Jesus advised is to tell them. The second is to go personally.

III. And the third step is to take some wise Christians with you. He puts it, "But if he does not listen, take one or two others along with you, that every word may be confirmed by the evidence of two or three witnesses." Deuteronomy 19:15 (KJV) has it: "One witness shall not rise up against a man for any iniquity or for any sin . . ." No doubt Matthew had that saying in mind.

But in this case you don't take others along to prove wrongdoing, but rather to help the reconciliation. It may well be that we are the ones, and not the other person, who are in the wrong! Hate often develops against those whom we have wronged or who have wronged us. It sometimes is so, that we just can't say or do the right thing to resolve the conflict ourselves. There are always those few saints who can work reconciliation. Jesus called them peacemakers."

If we talk things over with a wise person, that person can often help us see ourselves as others see us. The rabbis had a wise saying, "Judge not alone, for none may judge alone save one. (That is God)." The third step is to ask for help.

"Father forgive them," were Christ's words — words of sharp contrast to the words of the world. Louis Untermeyer in *Heinrich Heine: Paradox and Poet* describes the spirit of the world: "Forgiving was not Heine's business nor his specialty. 'My nature is the most peaceful in the world,' he wrote with deceptive mildness. 'All I ask is a simple cottage, a decent bed, good food, some flowers in front of my window, and a few trees beside my door. Then, if God wanted to make me completely happy, he would let me enjoy the spectacle of six or seven of my enemies dangling from those trees. I would forgive them all the wrongs they have done me — forgive them from the bottom of my heart, for we must forgive our enemies. But not until they are hanged.'"

IV. The fourth step — according to Jesus — is, if all that fails, we must take our personal troubles to the Christian fellowship.

It is so true that within the Christian fellowship, if it is Christian, conflicts can be resolved, if at all possible, by not going to law or by Christless argument. Legalism seldom settles relationship problems, but often drives them deeper.

What Jesus means here is this: It is in an atmosphere of Christian prayer, Christian love, and Christian fellowship that personal relationships may be righted. It is clear that Jesus makes a big assumption here that our fellowship is Christian, and that because of that, we judge everyone not on legalism, but in the light of love.

He puts it, "If he refuses to listen to them, tell it to the church."

So that's the fourth step, tell it to the church. The fifth follows right afterward ". . . if he refuses to listen even to the church, let him be to you as a Gentile and a tax collector." (Matthew 18:17)

V. The advice to treat him as a Gentile and a tax collector seems like very tough advice from Jesus. If you don't succeed, Jesus advises to treat the person as a Gentile and tax collector. The first impression here is to give up and treat the person as hopeless and abandon him or her as irreclaimable. However, Jesus never set limits to human forgiveness. Remember what he told Peter? We must forgive seventy times seven.

William Barclay reminds us in his commentary that when Jesus spoke of Gentiles and tax collectors, he always did so with sympathy and gentleness with an appreciation of their good qualities. "It may be that Jesus was saying something like this: 'When you have done all this, when you have given the sinner every chance, and when he remains stubborn, you may think he is no better than a tax collector and Gentile. Well, you may be right. But I have not found tax collectors and Gentiles hopeless. My experience of them is that they, too, have a heart that can be touched, and there are many of them like Matthew and Zacchaeus, who have become my best friends. Even if the person is like a tax collector and Gentile you can still win him, as I have done.'"

So this Scripture does not say to give up. In fact, it challenges us to win the heart — the hardest heart! It tells us that Jesus finds no person hopeless — and neither must we.

Reinhold Niebuhr, in *The Irony of American History*, writes, "Nothing that is worth doing can be achieved in our lifetime: therefore we must be saved by hope. Nothing which is true or beautiful or good makes complete sense in any immediate context of history; therefore we must be saved by faith. Nothing we do, however virtuous, can be accomplished alone, therefore we are saved by love. No virtuous act is quite as virtuous from the standpoint of our friend or foe as it is from our standpoint. Therefore we must be saved by the final form of love which is forgiveness."

Sure, we'll have conflicts within the discipleship, our congregation, the church. Sure, it'll be tough resolving them. But our Savior tells us ways we can do it; we should do it; we must do it — if ours is a Christian fellowship and we are Christian.

I. Tell the person about it.
II. See him or her in person.
III. Counsel with other wise Christians.
IV. Make use of the Christian fellowship
V. Never give up the try.

Seventeenth Sunday after Pentecost
Matthew 18:21-35

Forgiveness Unlimited

"Then Peter came to Jesus and asked, 'Lord, how many times can my brother sin against me and I have to forgive him? Seven times?'"

" 'No, not seven times,' answered Jesus, 'but seventy times seven.'" (Matthew 13:21-22) Big blundering Peter was always blurting out something! Every time he opens his mouth, according to the New Testament, he puts his foot in it. Yet, we can be thankful that Peter was that way. Better an over-enthusiastic Peter, than a cold, conniving Judas. Besides, the words that Jesus used to answer Peter's impetuous remarks and questions were often great words for us today.

No doubt about it, the big fisherman thought he was being over generous in suggesting he forgive seven times. He probably expected a compliment from Jesus for suggesting that he should be so patient and forgiving. Instead, Jesus surprised them all with his advice. "No, not seven times," answered Jesus, "but seventy times seven." (Matthew 13:22)

The rabbis taught that you should forgive your brother three times. Rabbi Jose ben Hanina said, "He who begs forgiveness from his neighbor must not do so more than three times." They worked this out from the book of Amos in the Old Testament. In the first chapters of Amos, there is a series of condemnations on the countries for three transgressions and for four. From this, they reasoned that God would forgive you three times; but, punishment would be given out on the fourth. They further reasoned that no person could be more forgiving than their God. So forgiveness was limited to three offenses.

No doubt Peter thought he was really offering to be very generous when he offered seven times. He expected to be praised for the generous seven times — instead Jesus' answer says there is no limit at all to God's forgiveness and no limit on a Christian's forgiveness — it is forgiveness unlimited.

A worker was shorted two dollars in his pay envelope, and complained to the paymaster. "You were overpaid two dollars last week and didn't object," reasoned the paymaster. "I know," said the employee, "I don't mind overlooking one mistake, but when it happens the second time, I think it's time to complain."

Jesus then tells the story of a man who was forgiven, but went out and refused to forgive someone who owed him a tiny fraction of what he had been forgiven. Jesus condemned the man without mercy. He said, ". . . That is how my father in heaven will treat you if you do not forgive your brother, every one of you, from your heart." (Matthew 18:35)

Here are several things which Jesus taught over and over. A person must forgive others to know forgiveness. That theme runs all through the New Testament. Forgive to be forgiven. We are told over and over — we will not be forgiven unless we forgive our fellow persons. We can't hope for God's forgiveness unless we forgive. "Happy are those who are merciful to others; God will be merciful to them." (Matthew 5:7) And in the great disciples' prayer, Jesus taught them: "If you forgive others the wrongs they have done you, your father in heaven will also forgive you. But if you do not forgive the wrongs of others, then your father in heaven will not forgive the wrongs you have done." (Matthew 6:14-15) James put it: "For God will not show mercy when he judges the man who has not been merciful; but mercy triumphs over judgment." (James 2:13)

They go together like bread and butter, like ham and eggs, like hand and glove. Divine, or God's forgiveness, and our forgiveness of each other belong together. To know forgiveness, we must forgive.

Clarence E. McCartney tells this story about forgiveness: During one of the persecutions of the Armenians by the Turks, an Armenian girl and her brother were pursued by a bloodthirsty Turkish soldier. He trapped them at the end of a lane and killed the brother before the sister's eyes. The sister managed to escape by leaping over the wall and fleeing into the country. Later she became a nurse. One day a wounded soldier was brought into her hospital. She recognized him at once as the soldier who had killed her brother and had tried to kill her. His condition was such that the least neglect or carelessness on the part of the nurse would have cost him his life. But she gave him the most painstaking and constant care. One day when he was on the road to recovery, he recognized her as the girl whose brother he had slain. He said to her, "Why have you done this for me, who killed your brother?" She answered, "Because I have a religion which teaches me to forgive my enemies."

There is a big difference between the two debts. The first person's debt was a whale of a lot of money. It would be equal to the budget of a small town in our day, an incredible debt — millions of dollars. The debt that the fellow servant owed was a tiny one compared to the first. A few dollars is what it is called in the *Today's English Bible*. In fact, it was approximately one five-hundred thousandth of the first debt. The contrast between the two debts is overwhelming. That's the point Jesus was making: Nothing that people can do to us can in any way compare with what we have done to God. If God is willing to forgive us all we owe him, we should be willing to forgive each other. Their debts to us are so small compared with what God has forgiven us. And let's remember always that Christians' forgiveness is always limitless.

During the Revolutionary War, at the town of

Ephrata there lived a very reputable and highly respectable citizen who had suffered an injury from a worthless and vile man in their town. This wicked man enlisted in the army, and there lived up to his evil record in civil life. Presently he was arrested for a serious offense, convicted by a court martial and sentenced to be hanged. The news of the sentence got back to Ephrata. Then that citizen whom this convicted man had wronged set out for the army, walking all the way to Philadelphia and beyond. When he found his way to Washington's headquarters, he pleaded for the life of this convicted man. Washington heard him through and then said he was sorry, but he could not grant the request. But seeing the disappointment in the man's face when he turned to go, Washington said, "Are you a relative of this man?" The man said, "No." "Then," said Washington, "are you his friend?" "No, that man was my deadly enemy."

Nothing that we must forget and forgive and let go is even remotely close to what God has had to overlook and forgive in us.

Not far from New York there is a cemetery which has inscribed upon a headstone just one word — "Forgiven." There is no name, no date of birth or death. The stone is unblemished by the sculptor's art. There is no epitaph, no fulsome eulogy — just that one word, "Forgiven," but that is the greatest thing that can be said of any person, or written upon one's grave, *"Forgiven."*

We have been forgiven much more than we could possibly ever repay. For our sins, for the sins of our sinful race, brought about God's son dying on a cross for our forgiveness. So that we might have relief and pardon and a clean slate, he went to Calvary. That means we have the opportunity to start over forgiven. When you get that kind of forgiveness, you are just compelled to make a part of that starting over the forgiveness of those petty little grievances with other people.

We get angry with that servant whose master

forgave him so much while he refused to forgive so little. Yet we are often like him. We nurse along a grudge, and we refuse to overlook a mistake, we keep warm a dislike or resentment, while the whole time Christ is stretched out on that cross that we might be forgiven.

Let's do two things about this Gospel today. Let's remember again all that our patient heavenly Father has done for us. Let's remember again Bethlehem, and Nazareth, and Galilee, and Jerusalem. Let's remember the cross and the agony, and whipping, and torment, and sweat, and blood, and suffering there. All this was done so the gift of forgiveness might be offered to us over and over again by a loving and patient Father. Then, when we have that firm and renewed in our mind, let's be about forgiving our fellow persons. And let us especially begin within our own fellowship of Christian believers. Let us not neglect our own family, mates, and those who live in our homes.

When Jesus said seventy times seven, Luke records the disciples as saying, "Make our faith greater." (Luke 17:5b) Seventy times seven is four-hundred ninety. We can do it in our heads, but this is God's arithmetic: we must "do it in our hearts." To little things we sometimes say: "Don't worry about it," or "Forget it." Those words don't mean big forgiveness. Here Jesus wants us to forgive those things that hurt, that gnaw away at us, that eat us up inside, and when it just isn't our fault. Sometimes we are like the man who said that he buried the hatchet, but remembered where he buried it!

Out of the great overflow and warm knowledge of what God has done and is doing for us, let us also forgive. Pick out someone to whom you will offer forgiveness today. Offer the hand and heart in love. Patch up the relationship, strengthen the friendship, set up the fellowship again. We are indeed the forgiven, the forgiving.

The Norwegian writer Johan Bojer, in *The Great Hunger*, tells of a man whose little child was killed by a neighbor's dog. Revenge would not long satisfy this man, so he found a better way to relieve the agony of his heart. When a famine had plagued the people and his neighbor's fields lay bare and he had no corn to plant for next year's harvest, the troubled father went out one night and sowed the neighbor's field, explaining: "I went and sowed seed in my enemy's field that God might exist."

Just as someone who has suffered grief can best give sympathy to those who grieve, just as a person who has lost his job can offer help to an unemployed person, just as someone who has been divorced can best help someone going through divorce, so we, who know what it is to have the tremendous weight of guilt and fear lifted up from us, can best lift it from another.

Let us rejoice in the way God has forgiven us. Let us forgive each other; and let us remember that we must forgive in order to be forgiven.

Eighteenth Sunday after Pentecost
Matthew 20:1-16

God's Generosity Resented

Here is the crazy story that Jesus told: A man owned a vineyard and needed to get the grapes harvested before the rains came. He hired some men at the early morning hour and agreed to pay them a silver coin for the day's work. At nine and noon, and then at five p.m., he hired more men to help with the harvest. When evening came, the owner called all the workers together. They were all paid the same amount. Those who worked ten hours were paid the same amount as those who worked one hour. Those who had worked all day began to complain. The owner told them they had no reason to complain — he paid them what they had agreed upon when they started. He then said, "Don't I have the right to do as I wish with my own money? Or are you jealous because I am generous?" (Matthew 20:15)

The story sounds as if it were a dreamed up tale; however, this sort of thing was real in Palestine. There, the grape harvest comes on in September very quickly, and must be harvested before the rain comes. It's a race against time to make it. Anybody who can work, does, even if he can work only an hour or two. The pay for a day's work was the average for that time. The men standing in the town square waiting for work was a similar scene to our union halls of today — very common in that part of the world. They would stand there with their equipment all day waiting for a job. The fact that some of them stood till five o'clock shows that they really wanted to work.

These people always lived on the poverty line. Whether they got a job or not determined if they and their families ate that day. To have no one hire them was a disaster. So this was a common sight and situation in Palestine, that all who heard Jesus would understand. It could be seen in any small town where the grape harvest was being rushed before the rains came.

There are some truths here that go right to the center of our Christian belief. When Jesus first told the story, it had a special significance to those who heard it. There is a warning here to the disciples who heard it. Jesus was telling them that they were very fortunate to be in on the beginning of the Christian movement. He warned them that there would be others who would join much later. He was warning them that they must be careful about thinking they are better than those who join later than they did.

Jesus was saying that all people, no matter when they come to Christ and his church, are precious in his sight. It is easy for us who have been in the church a long time, investing so much of ourselves in it, to feel we are above or better or more important to God than those who have joined recently.

Often when the young and "new blood" in the congregation want to change things, or begin to operate with different methods and procedures, we can come to resent it. We feel as though we have so much more invested in the congregation that things just ought to be done the way we are used to doing them. This story tells us that seniority does not so much mean honor as it does responsibility in the family of God.

Jesus was also speaking to the Jews. There is a strong warning here against exclusiveness. No doubt these Jews saw themselves as the chosen people, God's special folks — thus they looked down on the Gentile people. Jesus must have told this story to warn them that the Gentiles were also God's people. Even, though they come late, they still are rewarded the same gift.

Someone has said, "In God's economy, there is no such thing as a most favored nation clause."

One race, or one denomination, or one nationality is not more important to God than another. Let's put that on the billboards of our lives. There is no single franchise on God's grace. These two things Jesus must have wanted to say to the Jews and the disciples in his day when he told the story. But, when we study the Scripture, we must do more than discover its setting and its rationale back then; we must also ask ourselves, "What does this parable say to us now?"

Here we learn a lot about our God, and it's all very reassuring.

The story tells us that God is kind. To be unemployed is a devastating thing. It robs us of our sense of self-worth. It removes from us our pride and feelings of accomplishment. It degrades and embarrasses us. It is a tragic thing when our talents, our capability to do things is wasted and idle. In Shakespear's play *Othello*, a great line is "Othello's occupation is gone."

So here stood these men: sad, depressed, angry, and hurt. The owner of the vineyard took pity on them — he couldn't bear to see them idle — to think of them returning home with a tale of no employment and no income. So he hired them just for a brief time, and gave them the whole day's wages. He knew they couldn't return home with less, and still hold up their heads.

Henry Drummond used to say, looking back over a more than ordinarily distinguished life, that the things that stood out in this retrospect as an abiding worth and value were the four or five times he had reflected to others the kindness of God.

There is real kindness and compassion and tenderness in this picture of the owner of the vineyard.

Armin C. Oldsen writes: "Some years ago a well-meaning individual hit upon what he felt would be a sure-fire solution to the problems of the world. He would gather all the people in the world in a giant amphitheater and would read to them the story of the Good Samaritan, and tell them to '. . . go and do likewise,' that is to be kind to one another. I doubt it would do much good. I fervently wish, instead, it were possible to gather all the people of the world together in one place around the cross of Christ on Calvary. I would devoutly pray that while they were there, they might all be unforgetably impressed with the horror of the sin of humanity and with the boundless love of God in Christ."

William Barclay feels, "This parable states implicitly two great truths — the right of every man to work, and the right of every man to a living wage for his work."

I think it's a lot more profound than that — it pictures our God as concerned, caring about our welfare. When we are embarrassed, unable to support ourselves, feeling frustrated because of helplessness in our situation, God hurts for us and wants to help.

There is a basic kindness here that is beautiful.

There is also encouragement in this story. God comforts us. He reassures us that those who came into his kingdom at the very last moment still are dear and precious to him. Don't worry about the latecomer to the faith. God still loves and cares for him. Be encouraged — our God doesn't check your years of service — we have the great reward for them here.

When a missionary had told a Chinese mother about the love of God, the mother exclaimed: "I've always thought there should be a God like that."

It's encouraging, isn't it? He loves us — those who are baptized as infants, those who are confirmed, those who come to him at marriage, those who are baptized as adults, those who seek him out in tragedy, and those who at the last moment of their lives, finally give in to God.

He paints the lily of the field,
Perfumes each lily bell:
If He so loves the little flowers,
I know He loves me well.

Maria Straus

Then, too, people die at all ages — old and faithful for years and young and just beginning. From God comes the same open arms and welcome for both because of Jesus Christ. Neither died too early or too late.

Notice how generous God is. They who worked only part of the day got a real gift. It's true of God: the length and kinds of ways we serve him all rank the same — the preacher, the usher, the choir member, the calling member, the janitor, the one who witnesses on his job. Notice, too, you and I don't even earn a reward from God. He gives us an undeserved gift. What God gives is not salary, then, but a generous gift, not a reward, but his wonderful grace.

"Why did the earlier workers not rejoice that the man who had waited long in the marketplace was now at peace, with money to take home to his family? Why did not the older brother rejoice that the prodigal was now restored, set free from the rags and hunger of the far country? If only we had but a tincture of God's love would we not be glad, as heaven is glad, that the lost sheep is safe in the fold, delivered from briars and wolves? Or are you jealous because I am generous?' God asks." (*Interpreter's Bible* on Matthew)

It's tough to give up our idea of earning what God gives us! The lovelessness of these all day workers is set to contrast the generosity of God. The rewards of God just do not mesh with our human standards and way of thinking. But these men who worked all day were not cheated — instead, those who only worked for a short time received a gift.

There is something important here. The big difference in the workers is the spirit in which they do their work. Looking at it reasonably, those who worked all day had a legitimate gripe. The logical way of looking at it would say that they would be paid more than those who worked only a few hours. The difference was that the first who came, the Scripture says, had an agreement. The last ones merely worked because they were delighted to have a job and a chance to earn something. They were willing to leave the remuneration up to the master.

The big difference here is motivation. If we go about our work asking "What will I get out of it?", that's one reason to work. Another, is to do the work of the kingdom for the joy of working and the joy of serving our God and God's people.

A business block in a western city bears this motto: Service is the rent we pay for the space we occupy.

Archbishop Nathan Soderblom used to say, "Doctrine divides, but service unites."

The friends of Louis Pasteur reported the scientist as often saying, "In what way can I be of service to humanity? My time and energy belong to mankind."

Jesus ended his parable with these familiar words, "So those who are last shall be first, and those who are first will be last." (Matthew 20:16b) The person who goes about serving with no regard for the reward, but working for the joy of it, will know the joy of the Christian life — to aim at regard is to fail to achieve it, and to forget reward is to find it.

When the wife of the late Bishop Frederick Bohn Fisher took an Indian child up in her arms, she did not know that the burning body of the child was tortured with typhus; but three days later, she was dead. Her heartbroken husband wrote the tribute for the stone that marked her resting place: "She died serving."

Let us remember that the difference here is in the motivation to serve. Let us recall always that God is generous, and that God has encouragement for us. The story tells us that God is kind. We have a warning — to beware of being exclusive like the Jews, and beware of thinking that we who are a long time in the church, are more privileged than others.

"Don't I have the right to do as I wish with my own money? Or are you jealous because I am generous?" And Jesus concluded, "So those who are last will be first, and those who are first will be last." (Matthew 20:15-16)

Nineteenth Sunday after Pentecost
Matthew 21:28-32

When Yes Means No
and No Means Yes

What's your opinion? If you have two sons, and you tell one of them to do a job, and his answer is no, then afterwards he does it, and you tell the second one to do the same job and his answer is, "Sure, I'll go," and he doesn't do it, which one is doing what you told him and following your will?

That's the story Jesus told the crowd, and that's the question he posed to the religious leaders of his day. The crowd answered Jesus by saying the son who said, "No," and then changed his mind and did the work was better than the other son. Jesus said, "That's right," and he illustrated that by saying that the tax collectors and the harlots of the day would go into the kingdom of God before the Jewish religious leaders to whom he was speaking.

This parable was told for a special reason. Jesus was saying that the Jewish leaders were like the son who said "yes" that he would obey and then did not do it. Jesus is saying that the tax collectors and harlots are like the son who said "No," changed his mind, and finally ended up obeying. In our text it goes like this, "Truly I say to you, the tax collectors and the harlots go into the kingdom of God before you."

I don't like either son's behavior! Neither son would bring joy to me, if I were his father. That's the key to understanding this parable. Jesus is not praising either one.

Jesus holds in front of us two sets of imperfect people

of whom one set is no better than the other. Neither son was a joy to his father. Both were imperfect people; but one certainly pleased his father more than the other.

I personally wish Jesus had added a third son to his parable. I would have liked a son who listened to the request, agreed to do it, and did it at once with enthusiasm.

There are some important lessons for us in this story. This parable details for us two kinds of people: The one kind is those whose words are a lot better than their deeds, and the second kind is those whose deeds are a lot better than their words.

The first group is a devastating group to a congregation of believers! They say with their mouths that they believe — but their lives do not reflect it. A whole generation of young people can be turned off by our inconsistency, by our speaking piety and fidelity — but living by the world's priorities.

Edwin T. Settle in *Religion in Life* writes: When our division was sent to the California coast to do amphibious training, late one evening I was walking along the deck of a large army transport chatting with a Jewish medical officer. On his own initiative he started to talk about religion ... "You know," he said, "I admire the man whom that book describes more than any other man of whom I know. And I have tried to put into my life some of the principles he taught. But sometimes I'm puzzled. As I look around me, I find persons who call themselves Christian who, it seems to me, deny the principles this man taught. I wonder sometimes, if I am not more Christian than they are, even if I am a Jew."

How often we are flushed out as being this kind of phony Christian when we practice stewardship (or rather, fail to practice it.) We say that Christ is the most important thing in our lives. We say that the work of the kingdom is important. We pledge our allegiance to the Savior. But, when it comes right down to it — we act out a whole different set of priorities. Everything else comes first before we give our cash to Christ's church. Our own comforts and conveniences come way ahead of the family of God.

We just don't ring true — the words and promises we make about our Christ and his church don't speak nearly as loudly as our actions, which often say the opposite. We are indeed often like this man who says, "Yes, I'll do it," and then doesn't.

At confirmation, when we promise, "Yes, we'll be responsible for our baptism," when we are married at the altar and make those solemn vows, when we are installed as officers of the church, when we are received into the congregation of believers, when we accept responsibility on committees, and the many other times we make promises before God and to each other, we often are like this young man who says yes, but doesn't do the work.

Clarence E. Macartney tells: "When the Pennsylvania westbound train on which I was traveling stopped recently at Altoona before beginning the ascent on the mountains, I saw in the yards there many powerful engines, their bunkers filled with coal, steam up, smoke issuing from the stacks, fires glowing under the boilers, and engineer and fireman at their posts. The engines were ready to go into action. They had been fueled and fired, and manned for action — and they *did* go into action, pulling the long trains over the mountains.

"Too often in human life enthusiasm is aroused, emotion is stirred, noble goals are glimpsed, high priorities are entertained; but no action follows. Nothing is done about it. The splendid enthusiasms are wasted, the emotions are dissipated. The soul has not capitalized on what it desired, but did not will."

Perhaps the most devastating of all is the church member who says he'll do something in the church and then doesn't. Every congregation has a host of these "no show" volunteers who drag down the congregation's programs and the ministry of Christ in the community.

Yet one other thing about this Christian's life style. Not only does it present an insincere example of a Christian to others, not only does it drag down a congregation and its kingdom work, but it is a lousy self-image maker. We all know if the things we do match the things we say. We know if we are "phony" or sincere in the practice of the Christian faith. Even if we keep it a secret from everyone else and no one guesses, *we* know. We are going to think much better about ourselves and thus be better people if we practice what we preach and know it.

From Australia a few years ago came amazing stories of a kindly nurse who was doing wonderful things to enable children, who had been crippled with infantile paralysis, to walk. The name of Sister Elizabeth Kenny became known all around the world. Sister Kenny visited the United States and gave her treatments in several large hospitals. To one who spoke to her admiringly one day, Sister Kenny said quietly, "I'm no genius. I'm just a very ordinary person who still remembers and puts into action the stories my mother told me from the Bible." Sister Kenny had learned about Jesus, and had come to desire above everything else to live as he lived, and to love as he loved. That's the way Christ intends for us to live also.

Now let's look at the other son. He says, "No." And then the Scripture says he ". . . repented and went." While this is far from perfect, it is much better, isn't it? This son's story is often our story. We claim to be hard-boiled, hard-headed materialists, but secretly we have our hearts touched. We hope for more to life than this. Who among us has not been like this son who said no? But Jesus says, " . . . he repented . . ." Oh, how beautiful a father we have! We can change our minds. We can try again. We can have a change of heart.

We may have said no to the appeal for good stewardship, for the appeal to do the committee work of the church, the appeal to pledge, to tithe, to witness, to worship, to serve. How many times our answer, too, has been "No." But our heavenly father allows us to remain sons and daughters and continues to love us, and we can repent and do the deed.

During the war, brave people of the Danish underground had a motto: "Do it well, and do it now." What better motto could we have as Christians? Christian happiness lies not in merely knowing what Christ would want us to do, but in actually doing it!

This son faced the facts of life and conscience — he laid his pride aside, and he did that which he vowed he'd not do. I like him because he wasn't concerned about losing face among his peers and friends. Even though he'd vowed one thing, he was willing to swallow his pride and do the other that he realized was right.

Perhaps you, too, ought to consider, or reconsider, the request of service of the heavenly Father. Perhaps there are those "nos" that ought to be "yesses." If you have turned down the invitation to sing in the choir, make a stewardship pledge, to serve on a committee, to make a witness, to serve as a chairperson, to open your heart to Christ, to do the extra request of someone in the congregation, think of it now — consider changing, repenting — making your heavenly Father joyful.

The true friends of Christ are active. "Ye are my friends if you do . . . my commandments." Christ did not save us to sit down. As one has said, "The symbol of Christianity is not a rocking chair, but a cross."

A small boy in church with his parents listened to the minister describe his visit to a poor home. The minister pictured the bare rooms, the ragged clothing, the empty dishes on the table, the pale, hungry children. When he had finished his story, he announced the closing hymn. But the little boy, with tears in his eyes, cried out to his father, "But, Daddy, aren't we going to *do* anything about it?" That question is being asked by our Father over and over again — are we going to do anything about it?

Let's remember this — the real point of the parable is

that neither son is anything like perfect. The really good
Christian is the one whose actions and words match and
ring true.

William Barclay says in his commentary, "On the
other hand, this parable teaches us that a man can easily
spoil a good thing by the way in which he does it."

It's true, isn't it, that we can do some things very well
but ruin them in the way we do them? There are so many
examples of this in every Christian congregation. Again,
stewardship comes to mind. We can make our pledge, or
give our offering; but, not do it in a way that is attractive
to others. We can serve on a committee or work in the
church or share what we have, but do it in a begrudging
way. We have to be coaxed. Everyone who works with
us must be careful not to hurt our feelings. We must be
thanked over and over again. It is easy, indeed, to do the
right thing but in a way that makes it unattractive to
those around us.

We learn in this parable that the Christian way is not
only in performance and not promise, but also in doing
and responding in a gracious and loving and joyful
manner. Jesus summed it all up in a story recorded in
Matthew 21:28-32, "What do you think? A man had two
sons; and he went to the first and said, 'Son, go and work
in the vineyard today.' And he answered, 'I will not;' but
afterward he repented and went. And he went to the
second and said the same; and he answered, "I go, sir,'
but did not go. Which of the two did the will of his
father?"

Twentieth Sunday after Pentecost
Matthew 21:33-43

On Being a Tenant

All the details of the story that Jesus tells about being a tenant and owning a vineyard would have been familiar facts to the people who heard him tell it. I have on several occasions seen the vineyards of Israel, which are surrounded by a stone wall. On top of the wall is placed brambles that keep the wild animals from coming into the vineyard. They also protect the vineyard from thieves climbing over the stone wall. Many of the vineyards that I saw had a wine-press located right on the spot. A tower was usually built with the stones that were picked up to clear the vineyard, and that tower served as a place for a watchman to stand and observe the grapes as they were ripening, as well as a place to live for those who worked in the vineyard.

The behavior of the owner of this vineyard that Jesus talks about was also normal. In the time of our Lord, Palestine was a disturbed place, and held out little luxury for its citizens. It was quite often the case that a landlord would buy a vineyard, and then let out the vineyard and his farms to tenants, and travel to a country where living was better, and he could live off the income from his holdings in Palestine.

As a matter of fact, the actions of these tenants were not so uncommon either. In the time of our Lord, Palestine was seething with economic unrest. The working people were discontented and rebellious, and the action of the tenants in trying to get rid of the son was not by any means unimaginable.

It certainly would have been easy for all those who heard Jesus tell this story to understand what each element of the parable represented: the vineyard certainly represented the nation of Israel; the owner of the vineyard represented God; the tenants of the vineyard were the religious leaders of the day; the messengers who came to speak to the tenants were the prophets; and the son who finally came to appeal to the tenants was Jesus himself.

We can learn a lot about God by looking carefully at this story which Jesus told. There is something encouraging about the fact that God has a lot of trust in us people. In the story the owner of the vineyard trusted it to the tenants. He didn't stand over them and exercise a police-like supervision. In fact, he went away to another country and left them completely on their own. Isn't it a nice compliment that God trusts us with hs work in this fashion? Every job that we receive is a task that God would have us do.

This story also gives us a good look at the patience of God. Notice how the owner of the vineyard sent one messenger after another to appeal to the tenants. There wasn't any quick vengeance when the first messengers were abused or ill-treated. Notice that he gave the tenants many opportunities to respond to his appeal.

Robert Ingersoll, that great agnostic of a day gone by, once said to a contemporary, "I will give God five minutes to strike me dead for the things I have said." After five minutes and nothing had happened, Ingersoll's friend remarked, "Did you think you could exhaust God's patience in just five minutes?"

It's a great thing that God bears with us in all of our shortcomings and in all the ways that we disappoint him. He doesn't "chuck it" all and decide to obliterate us for our behavior. It is the very nature of God to make appeal after appeal to us and often through other people who are his messengers. Certainly we can see here a beautiful picture of the sadness of God as he watches life on our turbulent planet.

From the play *The Living Room*, by Graham Green,

we hear these words spoken: ". . . Do you imagine God doesn't see your problem and your suffering, and that he doesn't suffer with you just as you suffer . . . only worse? . . . He can't communicate with you, you won't let him . . . you don't trust him, and he suffers for that, too."

Goethe said: "If I were God, this world of sin and suffering would break my heart — and it did — on the cross." There is certainly in this story the element of God's judgment. At the end of the story the master of the vineyard took back his property and gave it to other people. I think we could say that it is often a judgment of God when he takes out of our hands the job we should be doing for him and must give it to someone else. We have gone to the lowest degree when we become useless to God like this.

Adam Clarke, the great biblical scholar of two hundred years ago, lies in Westminster Abbey. On his tomb is a candle, burned to near the socket, and around it these words: "In burning for others, I myself, also, have been consumed."

A man hurried to the church door one Sunday afternoon and said, "Is the service over?" An usher who had grasped the implicatons of the minister's words that day said, "The worship is over, but the service is only beginning." Certainly it is a judgment against us when we no longer make ourselves useful to our heavenly Father.

With keen insight, Jesus portrays us sinners as God's tenants of his vineyard. We see what a great privilege it is to be a tenant of God, and have all this given to us. The vineyard was a great one. They had everything they needed — hedge, winepress, the tower — which would have made it comparatively easy for those tenants and could have made possible their doing a very good job. It's good to know that God not only gives us certain tasks to accomplish in our life-time, but he also provides for us the means to get them done. In what a generous vineyard our lives are set!

We in the church are so often like these cultivators. We twist things around to where our whole way of looking at Christ and his church is "what they can do for me." We're angry if this or that isn't done for us the way we want it done. Shouldn't we rather concentrate on the privilege that is ours to live here, to be a member here, to have an opportunity to serve in this place? Most of us have a beautiful church building, a parish education unit, and all the equipment necessary to do God's work in his vineyard in a community. What is terrible is that we often let these facilities rust away rather than be used to the utmost for God's purpose. We often think of our church facilities and all the equipment that we surround ourselves with as a great privilege rather than a responsibility for their use. Our lives have been set in a gracious vineyard, and that's a privilege. We ought to look at our community and our church in the frame of mind that says, "How can I properly respond to this great privilege given me?" Rather than ask how well we might be entertained, and how well the church tickles our fancy, we ought to be concerned about how well we are serving the Christ of the church because we are privileged to be in his vineyard.

Did you notice here the human freedom that the tenants have? The master left those tenants and went away and allowed them to do their job as they liked and when they liked. It's good to know that our God is no tyrannical task master. He is like a wise leader who delegates authority to those who follow, and then trusts them to carry it out. In fact, God allows us to refuse many of his requests of service.

There is, of course, the element of accountability, too. That means that certainly God expects us to answer, as he did the tenants, as to how well we have used what he has given us. To every person there comes this day of reckoning. Paul wrote in Romans 14:12 "So, you see, each of us will have to answer for himself." So many are counting on a religious wife, or mother, to get them through, but this parable tells us that each person must give an account of how his use of God's vineyard has been carried out. Our life is ours, but only when we produce the fruits that God has asked us to produce.

Notice that in this parable the tenants are deliberate in their rebellion and disobedience towards the master. Sin is deliberate opposition to God, just like that. It is when you and I take our own way, rather than take the way which we know quite well God would have us take. These tenants decided to take things into their own hands, just as we often do, and did what they pleased with it.

You can't help seeing the stewardship implications in this story. We are often like those tenants. We are tenants living in God's vineyard with service to render to him, and because we have been given such a great garden, we must see it all as belonging to him and our responsibility to share it with him. We often treat the church as if we are doing it a favor when we give. Still, this parable would tell us that we Christians are obligated to return a considerable portion of all that God has given us from the vineyard. "Not what you possess, but what you do with what you have determines your true worth," said Thomas Carlisle.

God is indeed our landlord, and it all belongs to him. How about it? Do you say to a landlord, "You're always asking for your rent"? "No, I won't pledge what I will give you next year." "I'm not going to share the crop with you this year because I don't like one of your workers." The whole matter of stewardship is what relationship we think we have with God. Here Jesus says that we are like a tenant and a landlord — a landlord who loves us so dearly that he gives his only son to convince us of that love.

Let's look at that landlord's son who finally comes and makes the great appeal. Jesus lifts himself out of the succession of the prophets. Those who went before him were the messengers of God: no one can deny them that honor; but they were only servants. Here comes the son. The only son always has a special impact and appeal. This parable makes a clear claim that Jesus was unique; and to be unique from even the greatest of those who went before you is quite a claim!

The fact that our Lord told this parable makes it clear that he knew what lay ahead of him. The wicked men killed the son in the story. Jesus was never in any doubt that that would be his fate one day. He did not die because of some freak crowd eruption, or because he was compelled to; he went willingly and open-eyed knowing that it was what he must do for us. No other appeal had worked before or would work in the future. Alfred Adler, a psychologist and a Jew, in answer to the question of a Los Angeles pastor, "What do you think of Jesus Christ?" said, "Whenever I hear his name, I stop for reverence to the greatest character of human history."

If Jesus can call forth such a response from a Jew, certainly we who are Christians, and tenants of his abundance, ought respond in a greater fashion.

Leslie D. Weatherhead has declared: "Life will work only one way, and that is Christ's way. There is a precipice at the end of every other road. Broken, bruised, disillusioned, despairing, we know then that of ourselves and in ourselves there is no hope of finding anything but the hell of despair. I wish I could persuade the listener of that before he finds it out for himself."

We certainly have a lot to learn from this story about our freedom and what a responsibility and privilege that is. And then it tells us Jesus has a certain claim on us because of the sacrifice he made for us. The parable ends with a picture of the stone. Jesus said that the stone which the builders had discarded became the most important stone of all. The picture comes from Psalms 118:22: "The stone which the builders rejected is become the headstone of the corner." Originally the

Psalmist was talking about the nation of Israel; and in this parable certainly Jesus meant that even though we tried to reject Christ, refuse him, even tried to eliminate him, we sooner or later find that the Christ we rejected is the most important person in all the world. Our Savior is the foundation-stone upon which everything is built, and like a cornerstone in a magnificent building, he holds everything together. To refuse his way is to batter one's head against the walls of the law of God. To reject and turn him down is in the end to be crushed out of life. He promises in this parable that he comes to us with a loving appeal, God's only son, that we might receive him and know a new life as a tenant in his vineyard. On this you can build a meaningful existence.

And that's what it's like to be a tenant in God's world.

Twenty-First Sunday after Pentecost
Matthew 22:1-14

An Invitation to a Feast

Did you ever hear such a story? The Gospel for the day tells it: a man gave a marriage feast and no one showed. He sent his servants out and found everyone too busy. Some even treated his servants badly when they were invited. So he went out into the streets and dragged in anyone who would come, and finally the wedding reception was full. To those who heard the story from Jesus' own mouth, there was special meaning: The guests who had been invited and didn't come were the Jewish people. They had been invited by God years ago to be his chosen family, and yet when God's son came into the world they turned down the invitation. The result was that God invited those who had not originally been his chosen people, who never even expected an invitation into the Kingdom of God in the first place. The way the writer of Matthew saw it, the consequences of refusing this invitation were terrible. Verse 7 tells how the king sent his army against those who refused. That particular verse was not a part of the original Scripture. We can probably explain that by remembering that Matthew wrote about A.D. 80 and just ten years before that time Jerusalem had been destroyed by the Roman army. The temple was completely razed and the city was leveled. Disaster had come to those who had refused to recognize the Son of God when he came.

Some feel that if the Jews had accepted Christ and his teachings, they would never have been the rebellious, warring people who finally provoked Rome to come in and smash them.

It would be a mistake just to look at this parable in light of what it said to the people who heard it for the first time. Let's carefully consider what this Gospel has to teach us in our own lives and on this day.

The invitation that God gives to us is one to a feast as happy as a wedding reception or a rehearsal dinner. The invitation God gives us is a joyous one. If we think of Christianity as some kind of gloomy giving up of everything which brings laughter and sunshine and happy fellowship to life, we have the mistaken idea about our faith. It is to joy that we are invited by our king. It is joy that we miss if we refuse and do not attend the banquet. Jesus was the kind of person who often withdrew for prayer and meditation; but a great majority of his ministry was in the "swing of things." He went to wedding receptions. He attended banquets of sinners. He took part in parties that the Pharisees held. Christ broke the dismal, religious laws of the temple and the Hebrew people. He often celebrated with those folks as well as suffered and mourned with them. Jesus never pictured God as a tyrant who had to be appeased by long, sour faces and dismal refrains that looked suspiciously upon anything happy.

So we see that the invitation that we receive from God to the feast is a happy one. A woman arrived late for a wedding. As she came rushing up to the door, an usher asked her for her invitation. "I have none," she snapped. "Are you a friend of the groom?" he asked. "Certainly not!" the woman replied, "I'm the bride's mother." You and I are invited to a wedding feast of joy, and we are the friends of the king. Once Winston Churchill received an invitation from George Bernard Shaw to one of his opening plays back in the early 1900's. The note read, "Enclosed are two tickets to the performance of a play of mine. Bring a friend — if you have one." Churchill sent back this reply: "Dear GBS, I thank you very much for the invitation and tickets. Unfortunately, I am engaged on that night, but could I have tickets for the second night? — if there is one."

Let's be honest and admit that the things which make us ignore the invitation of Christ aren't always bad in themselves. These people did not go off on some wild or immoral adventure. When Luke tells this same story, he tells us that one person went to check on his real estate, another on his livestock and business, and another had family affairs that kept him away. These are all legitimate reasons for being absent. It is so easy to be so busy with the things of time, that we forget the things of eternity. We can become so preoccupied with the things which are seen that we forget the things that are unseen, to hear so often the claims of the world that we cannot hear the soft invitation of the voice of Christ to his banquet. Isn't it often true that the thing which is second best in our lives shuts out the very best? Those things which are good in themselves often shut out the things which are supreme. Probably the biggest competition for our loyalty to church and our Savior and living the Christian life is good causes in the community and in our lives, but not the best. Our involvement in social groups, in lodges, our elaborate vacations, recreation, television programs, and even our job, are certainly good reasons for arranging our priorities. We can be so busy making our living that we forget to make the most fulfilling life possible. It's an easy temptation to give our energy and our cash and our loyalty to the second best cause, rather than the supreme cause which is Christ and his church.

For those who turned down the king in the story, their reasons were pretty good. A yoke of oxen was very important back then, was almost a big business. Marriage was considered of high priority, and in fact, a person could be justified in losing two week's profit for the honeymoon. To purchase a farm was of extreme importance. Merchandise is important. All these things have much significance to our livelihood. The trouble is, those things important to livelihood can sometimes usurp the very throne of life itself.

Next time you're some place where people have opportunity to talk a lot, listen closely to the conversations. I mean places like barber shops, filling stations, beauty salons, and school dormitories. You'll hear conversations about cars, taxes, sports, houses, boats, and sex. But if one of the people wants to discuss human destiny or the claims of Christ on our lives, invariably that person will be thought of as odd, and the rest will shuffle their feet in discomfort.

Nevertheless, we do have an invitation from Christ to his feast. Mrs. Jones was reading a letter at breakfast. Suddenly she looked up suspiciously at her husband. "Henry, I've just received a letter from Mother saying she isn't accepting our invitation to come and stay, as we do not appear to want her. I told you to write and tell her she was to come at her own convenience. You did write, didn't you?" "Er, — yes — I did," said the husband, "but I couldn't spell convenience so I made it risk."

I like this invitation from the King because it tells us very much about the kind of invitation Christ issues to *us*. He doesn't try to frighten us with hell to get us to come to the banquet. Rather, he appeals to us with this story of all those who did not come and what they missed because of their refusal. If we refuse the invitation we are some day going to be heart-sick when we realize what we missed all those years. We will know then that we have cheated ourselves out of a rich and fulfilling life.

We still have the "burn in hell" scare technique used by preachers — but that's not the way that Christ appealed to us. His appeal was always "how much more." He always said to us that we could have a better, fulfilled existence if we accepted his invitation.

You and I have a great banquet prepared for us. God invites us to come and celebrate with him. The door is open, the invitation issued. We must not allow anything to get in our road. A feast of love and companionship and peace and security is ours. God wants us to have it. He pleads with us to please come.

If you have held back, really not given in, not surrendered to Christ and his church, if so far you've just been a wary spectator, a feast is waiting for you — the banquet is ready. This invitation isn't just for outsiders and unbaptized and unchurched people; we who have been members of the congregation all our lives are especially invited to finally and completely answer the invitation and come in to the feast in a new committed relationship to our Savior.

I implore you; remove the excuses, give up the reservations, don't hold back any longer. Open your hearts to Christ and say "yes" to the invitation. There is a new and exciting life waiting for you if you'll just come in. It's an invitation to a feast and you're the one invited!

This parable says in its last analysis that God's invitation to us is the invitation of Grace. This isn't an awards banquet. Those who were gathered in from the hedges and highways had no claim on the king at all — they could not have, by any stretch of the imagination, expected an invitation. Still less, could they have deserved it. This invitation came to them because the king was a wide-armed, open-hearted, generous, hospitable kind of person. And that's the kind of God who invites us. It was grace which offered the invitation and grace which gathered the people in.

In Eugene O'Neill's play, *The Great God Brown*, Brown says, "Man is born broken. He lives by mending. The grace of God is glue!"

Mary Ellen Chase, in *The Lovely Ambition*, chapter 4, writes this: "Grace?" he said. "Grace? Well, that's very difficult to explain, Mrs. Gowan. Many learned men have thought about grace for many centuries. Most of them think it has to do with forgiveness and mercy, but I'm inclined to disagree with them. I rather think grace means just the constant presence of God."

That's why we come to the banquet. Because God is continually present with us, and sees us through, and we accept his gracious invitation to be with him.

There is a second little parable added to this one to explain the responsibility of accepting the invitation:

"The king went in to look at the guests and he saw a man who was not wearing wedding clothes. 'Friend, how did you get in here without wedding clothes?' the king asked him. But the man said nothing. Then the king told the servants, 'Tie him up hand and foot and throw him outside in the dark. There he will cry and gnash his teeth.' And Jesus concluded, 'For many are invited, but few are chosen.' " (Matthew 22:11-14)

The first parable tells us about the open invitation to come to the feast, and how we as Gentiles and sinners who do not deserve it are gathered in. This parable tells us that it is true that the door is open to all people, but when we come in, we must bring with us a life which seeks to fit the love that has been given us. This kind of gracious invitation is not only a gift, but also a tremendous responsibility.

This second parable tells us that if, and when, we accept the wonderful gift, we must change our lives and work at being worthy of this kind of love of the God who has given us the invitation. This parable has nothing to do with the kind of clothing we wear to church, but it has everything to do with the kind of life we show as an example in the community where we live. When we come into the wedding feast of our God, we must put on the clothing of mind and heart and soul that is responsible and responsive to the gift that has been given us. When we come to the feast, we must come in all humility, with our profound faith, sorry for the kind of life we have lived, and with a deep sense of reverence as we come into his presence at the banquet. If we indeed come expecting great things to happen to us, and longing for the deep, warm fellowship of the believers at the banquet, that's what we'll find. If we come in the frame of mind which looks for dissatisfactions and complaints, we'll find plenty of those as well.

Jenny Lind always spent a few minutes alone in her dressing room before a concert. Her maid, who locked the door and stood guard, has told what happened in those last moments of preparation. Miss Lind would stand in the middle of the floor, her shoulders back, and her head up, draw a deep breath, strike a clear, vibrant note, and hold it as long as her breath lasted. When the overtones had all died away, she would look up and say: "Master, who has given me this undeserved gift, let me ring true tonight."

When we realize what a gift this invitation to God's kingdom is to us, we too will try our best to ring true. We have been invited to a grand feast of worship today, and as we come, our lives ought to be changed. If we come prepared to worship, ready for prayer, conscious of our sins, then worship will be worship indeed.

Well, that's the story that Jesus told about a king who invited people to a wedding feast and none came. He went out into the streets and gathered in those who didn't deserve the invitation. After the guests finally arrived, he demanded that they be responsible for the undeserved gift of the invitation in the first place. God asks no more and no less of us. You are invited today to the feast of our king.

Twenty-Second Sunday after Pentecost
Matthew 22:15-21

Double Citizenship

Jesus had attacked the orthodox Jewish leaders by telling the story of the two sons. (Matthew 21:28-32) The Jewish leaders are the son who did not do the father's will. Then he told the story of the wicked husbandmen (Matthew 21:33-46). Again, the religious leaders are the bad guys! In the story of the King's feast (Matthew 22:1-14), they are the condemned guests who turn down the invitation.

In the Scripture for today, we see the Jews launching their counterattack — they go at him by asking him embarassing questions in public. The Pharisees ask, "Tell us, then, what you think. Is it lawful to pay taxes to Caesar, or not?"

In debate we would call this a dilemma question. If he said that they should not pay it, they would report him to the government. If he said that he should pay it, the people would be angry. He would be a traitor. They would be angry because taxes were as sore a point with them as they are with us! Palestine was an occupied country.

There were three taxes the Romans extracted from these people:

1. A ground tax — a man must pay to the government one-tenth of his grain and one-fifth of the oil and wine which he produced.

2. An income tax — one percent of a person's income.

3. A poll tax — every male person from age fourteen to sixty-five and every female from age twelve to seventy-five must pay this which amounted to one denarius or one day's wages.

54

The tax here in question was this poll tax — one day's wages a year.

The Jews resented the tax, not just because we all hate taxes, but because to a few, God was the only king. To pay taxes to an earthly king was to admit the validity of his kingship and thus insult God.

Notice something else here — verse 15 tells us that the Pharisees and Herodians joined forces to attack Jesus. These are really strange bedfellows! It would be similar to the John Birch Society people and the Socialist Party people joining forces. The Pharisees were the super-religious who would resent very much the payment of taxes to a foreign king as an insult to their god. The Herodians were loyal to Herod, King of Galilee, who had joined the Romans and owed their power to them. They forgot their differences for a while and joined together to attack Jesus. They both wanted to eliminate him. Any person who is self-centered, concerned only about himself and his own power, will hate Jesus and want to get rid of him.

Remember Matthew wrote this story in a day when the temple had been destroyed and Jews were forced to pay the temple tax anyhow. The tax went to Temple Jupiter in Rome. It's easy to see that the matter of taxes was a real problem during Jesus' life on earth and during the life of the early church when this Gospel was written and read.

Jesus asked to see a coin — " 'Show me the money for the tax.' And they brought him a coin. And Jesus said to them, 'Whose likeness and inscription is this?' They said, 'Caesar's.' "

In those times, as soon as a king began to rule, he had his own coinage issued, and that coinage was held to be the property of that king. Jesus said that if Caesar's picture is on the coin, it is his, and so give it to him. "Render therefore to Caesar the things that are Caesar's, and to God the things that are God's."

So here is a great principle laid down by Jesus. A

Christian, a disciple of Jesus, is a person with double citizenship.

We are citizens of the country and world in which we live, and we are fortunate to live here!

Earl Warren said, "I believe no one can read the history of our country without realizing that the Good Book and the Spirit of the Savior have from the beginning been our guiding geniuses . . . Whether we look to the first Charter of Virginia . . . or to the Charter of New England . . . or to the Charter of Massachusetts Bay . . . or to the Fundamental Orders of Connecticut . . . the same objective is present: a Christian land governed by Christian principles . . . I believe the entire Bill of Rights came into being because of the knowledge our forefathers had of the Bible and their belief in it. Freedom of belief, or expression, or assembly, or petition; the dignity of the individual, the sanctity of the home, equal justice under law, and the reservation of power to the people . . . I like to believe we are living today in the spirit of the Christian religion. I like also to believe that as long as we do so, no great harm can come to our country."

To our country we owe a lot! We benefit from all the public services: law and order, government, fire protection, streets, water, education, Social Security and old age benefits. That means we have responsibilities to our country, community, and our state. That in turn means that Christians are obligated to be good citizens. When we have a debt, we must meet it. When we have an obligation, we keep it. When we make a commitment, we are good for it. Whatever we do, we do well; so because we live in the world, in the community, in the state, we should do our part and take our responsibilities seriously.

In an invocation prayer at the United States Senate, Peter Marshall said, "Lord Jesus, Thou who art the way, the truth, and the life, hear us as we pray for the truth

56

that shall make men free. Teach us that liberty is not only to be loved but also to be lived. Liberty is too precious a thing to be buried in books. It costs too much to be hoarded. Make us to see that our liberty is not the right to do as we please, but the opportunity to please to do what is right."

It is unthinkable that a Christian would not vote! It is unthinkable that Christians would not run for public office! It is unthinkable that Christians would withdraw from the responsibility of taking part in public life. The Christian has a responsibility to Caesar for all the privileges which the rule of Caesar brings. We are citizens of this world and must be good ones, if we are Christ's disciples.

On the court house of Cuyahoga County in Cleveland, Ohio, are inscribed these words: "Obedience to Law is Liberty." One of the judges pointed out that there is a significant omission in the inscription. It comes from Richard Hooker, the 16th Century author and stylist, and what Hooker wrote was this, "Obedience to *divine* law is liberty."

And that brings us to the second citizenship in our double citizenship: not only are we citizens of this world — but our citizenship is double, we are citizens of heaven.

Because God is our final allegiance, because God is our creator, our final authority, our top loyalty is to our God. When our citizenship in this world clashes with the will of our God — it is God's will that must be done. So we not only are citizens, we are also the *conscience of our government* — we have an extra responsibility in our citizenship.

Charles L. Wallis wrote: "For many years the famous and now fortunately discarded motto which a leading newspaper blazoned across its editorial masthead, 'My country, right or wrong!' was the accepted philosophy of too many patriotic Americans. Today the truly patriotic American accepts John Sutherland Bonnell's revised version: 'My country, when wrong, to be made right; when right, to be kept right.' "

When we are sure something is God's will, we must see that it is held up before our country and done. When we are sure that something is contrary to God's will, we must resist, oppose, bring our influence to bear, that it shall not be done.

J. B. Priestly once said: "We should behave toward our country as women behave toward the men they love. A loving wife will do anything for her husband except stop criticizing and trying to improve him. We should cast the same affectionate, but sharp, glance at our country. We should love it, but also insist on telling it all its faults. The noisy, empty patriot, not the critic, is the dangerous citizen."

A good citizen — here is the truth Jesus tells — is both a good citizen of his country *and* of the Kingdom of God. He will serve both his fellow persons and his creator God. As Peter puts it, "Fear God, and honor the king." (1 Peter 2:17)

There is often a fine line between the two kingdoms — the two areas of loyalty and responsibility, and our conscience must here enlighten us and be our guide.

Thomas Jefferson, a serious student of the Bible, wrote: "I always have said, and always will say that the studious perusal of the sacred volume will make better citizens, better fathers and better husbands."

I doubt that Jesus was trying to give us here for all time the relationship between church and state. He was dealing with a specific situation at a specific time in history. We must apply the principles and implications for our time with the help of God's spirit. Our participation in community must be as prayerful and holy as our participation in the church and the holy sacraments. We must not divide everything in our lives into holy and secular; but, rather, bring to bear the holy in our daily routine, our responsibilities of this life.

W. B. Selah says: "A certain dairyman objected to having his cows inspected for tuberculosis and ran the

58

Good Illustration

inspector off with a shotgun. In justification of his drastic action, he said, 'I am free, white, and twenty-one, and no government official is going to tell me how to run my business.' He forgot something. He forgot that his freedom to sell milk ends where the rights of babies to health begin. He needed to be told: 'Ye have been called into liberty; only use not your liberty for an occasion to the flesh, but by love serve one another.' Without a keen sense of social obligation, liberty is dangerous."

Jesus said to these Jews: "Pay the tax; it is their coinage that has brought some benefits. Revolution will only make things worse for you." As a matter of fact, the Jews did not take Jesus' advice, and there was a great deal of bloodshed as a result.

It began as an attempt to trap Jesus with a dilemma question. It ended up with a beautiful lesson for all times, for all Christians, on our double citizenship: in this world, to our country; and in the Kingdom of God to our Savior. As disciples, we bring these together as our Christian life style in our great democracy called America.

Harry Emerson Fosdick put it: "We Americans say that the Constitution made the nation. Well, the Constitution is a great document, and we never would have been a nation without it, but it took more than that to make the nation. Rather, it was our forefathers and foremothers who made the constitution and then made it work. The government they constructed did get great things out of them, but it was not the government primarily that put the great things into them. What put the great things into them was their home life, *their religion*, their personal sense of responsibility to a mighty God, their devotion to education, their love of liberty, their personal character. When their government pumped, it drew from profound depths in the lives of men and women where creative spiritual forces had been at work."

Twenty-Third Sunday after Pentecost
Matthew 22:34-40

Love of God, Self, and Neighbor

The religious people of Jesus' day got together to try to trap Jesus with their questions. They asked him about paying taxes. They asked him about rising from death. We read today that they asked him what was the greatest commandment. The Jewish rabbis liked to distill the meaning of religion into little phrases like the ones we put on our Burma Shave signs. They had six hundred thirty-two laws and rules for the practice of their religion. They tried to break it down into a couple of inclusive commandments.

"Teacher," he asked, "which is the greatest commandment in the law?" Jesus combined two commandments from the early Hebrews and put them together: the shema — Deuteronomy 6:4 and the great command in Leviticus 19:18 were combined. Together they go: "You must love the Lord your God with all your heart, with all your soul, and with all your mind . . . you must love your fellow man as yourself." (Matthew 22:37 & 39)

For Jesus, religion distilled into three things: love of self, love of God, and love of other people. Let's look at them one at a time and see their significance for our day and our practice of Christianity.

We must love ourselves. . . . "You must love your fellow man as yourself." (Matthew 22:39b) One of the messages of the New Testament and Jesus' ministry we often miss is that we are to have love for ourselves. In the Old Testament we read how God created us like him. "Then God said, 'Let us make man in our image and after our likeness . . . so God created man in his own image.' "

Betty Lombard joined our Lutheran Church in Tiffin when I was its pastor. She first came searching for meaning in her life to my Bible Study group. She had been in and out of Tiffin State Hospital a number of times. I baptized her and became her pastor and counselor. She would tell me how bad she was and what a rotten person she had been. I tried, in my simple way, to assure her that she was one of God's creations. One day she called me on the phone and told me she had a title for a sermon — I should preach on "love yourself." Five days later, they found Betty dead on her kitchen floor. She had committed suicide by slashing her wrists. She just could not accept the fact that she was good and God-made.

In an average year in the United States, 22,000 people kill themselves, and 100,000 more try. The real cause for such attempts, say the psychiatrists, is a sense of guilt and a desire to punish oneself. G. K. Chesterton calls the great lesson of "beauty and the beast" that a thing must be loved before it is loveable. If we are God's creation, and if we are created like God, we must think well of ourselves. We are well-made, we are God's handiwork, we are created like our Creator. There is an important message here — we are to love ourselves. In a day when self-worth is low, in a time when so much introspection is encouraged, and when human nature is looked at with suspicion, we need to say boldly — we are God-made! And let's remember, God makes us well. It would be blasphemy to hate ourselves since God is our Creator.

You've read in the newspapers about a whole community turning out to find a lost child. Hundreds of people gathered around a mine shaft while they searched for a lost miner. A whole nation watches and prays while one policeman is held hostage. We have the same kind of lavish attention focused on us by God.

There is something sacred about life — any life. If people would turn out a whole community to find a lost child, or dig out a lost miner, think how much more concern God has about each of our lives. And think about this: Think what a price God paid for us! We are so important to him that he sent his Son to save us. Think how the great events of our worship emphasize that fact — how at Christmas we celebrate his coming in the person of Jesus at Bethlehem, how we observe his growing up in Nazareth, how during Lent we look towards his going to Jerusalem and Calvary and the cross, how at Easter we celebrate his coming out of the tomb, and how on Ascension Day we observe the way he returned to his heavenly father — all this to demonstrate how important we are.

In dealing with ourselves, we are not dealing with rubbish; we are dealing with precious pieces of well-made machinery, copied after the Creator of the universe. When we finally stop putting ourselves down and respect who and what we are, there are many side benefits: we can much better be able to live with others; we have a new-found peace with ourselves; we can better live with ourselves because we are often our own worst enemies; we can bounce back from depression over divorce or disappointment in a love affair; we can handle almost anything life deals out when we fully realize that we are God-made, and God-saved, and God-loved.

Roy Pearson writes, "He has a work for me to do in the world, and in the doing of that work, you simply have no place. Your talents and assets have no more fitness for my task than mine have for yours, and both my peace of mind and my effectiveness in God's plan depend not upon my rejecting myself, repudiating myself, hating myself, but upon my accepting myself, rejoicing in myself, using myself."

Shakespeare had his actor say, "Self love, my liege, is not so vile a sin as self-neglecting."

To believe this means we'll decide things differently. How we treat our bodies takes on great significance.

Whether we use drugs or alcohol becomes important. How we neglect or abuse ourselves that God has created is a high priority. Whether we smoke or overeat are other decisions. All these become theological religious issues because we are dealing with a God-made, God-loved body.

Jesus said, "You must love your fellow man as yourself." That brings us to the second element in our text. We are not only to love ourselves, but we are to love God.

We are to love God. "You must love the Lord your God with all your heart, with all your soul, and with all your mind." (Matthew 22:37) This means we give our full commitment to God. It calls for us to have a total love which dominates and directs our thoughts and actions. We are created for love and worship. We are made to pour ourselves into a cause. We are created to give out — to love with whole self. Jesus says, ". . . with *all* your heart, with *all* your soul, and with *all* your mind." (Matthew 22:37b)

A columnist writing in the *Chicago Daily News* commented on a recent interview with the Secretary of the Army concerning the scandal at West Point in which one hundred fifty-one cadets were dismissed for having violated the academy's moral code against cheating. The Secretary, in discussing the cause of the scandal, reported that "at least two-fifths of the cadets of the classes of '76 and '77 at West Point when asked what the causes were, brought up removal of mandatory chapel." The Secretary was amazed. "Who among us would have thought of this effect of removing chapel? . . . They (the cadets) felt that sanctity was driven out of the moral code." The *Daily News* writer observed that it is hard for societies to have institutional morality when the individual does not have a personal morality based on some kind of personal belief. We need to love God — our very loving shapes our life-style and morals and gives content to our ethical decisions.

A partial devotion is a miserable way to live. It is destructive to hear one thing in church from Scripture and secretly do another. Some try just worshiping God with their emotions. They are afraid to use their brains. They believe you must check your brains at the church door when you join. Others try an intellectual religion but don't really feel Christ's presence with them. They know the facts about our Lord, but do not know him personally. And, of course, this command to love God is only possible in God's love. "We love because he first loved us." (1 John 4:19)

All religion begins here — loving our God totally — a complete commitment to him — with our energy, our cash, our self, emotions, talents, time, and brains.

To try to straddle life with a double loyalty — the things of the world having equal or more importance than the love of God — causes us emotional schizophrenia. That kind of cleavage in personality is tragic — our mental health is at stake as well as our spiritual well-being. The worst danger is when we try to do a little of each. If we ever, as a Family of God, took seriously loving God with our whole self, we would be something to behold! Everyone in the congregation would be an evangelist — we'd be receiving hundreds into this congregation's membership each couple of months. Everyone would be tithing — we'd have so much in the offering that we would have to put on extra counters to tabulate it, and find new ways to share it. All decisions and projects and work and activities of each organization of this church would measure and motivate what it did by asking if this is the best way to love God. Four thousand would be in church each Sunday. We wouldn't have room enough for all the Church School classes to study the Scripture.

As when a teen-ager falls in love, and everything he or she does revolves around the one he or she loves, so too with us; we love God, we love ourselves.

We must also love our neighbors. . . . "You must love

your fellow man as yourself." (Matthew 22:39b) When this rule was first given to the Pharisees, it came from Leviticus 19:18, and meant that they should love their fellow Jews. Jesus gave this a new interpretation with his story of the Good Samaritan. We are now to love all people, and especially those who need our love. It is surely true that in order to love well our neighbor, we must first love our God, love ourselves, and then we are capable of loving others. The bigot, the racially prejudiced, the hate-monger is always the person who has a low opinion of himself or herself. Religion for Jesus was loving self, God, and neighbor. He would put more teeth in that and said the *only* way we can show we love God is by loving others.

Lewis L. Austin, in *This I Believe*, wrote: "Our maker gave us two hands. One to hold onto him and one to reach out to his people. If our hands are full of struggling to get possessions, we can't hang onto God or to others very well. If, however, we hold onto God, who gave us our lives, then his love can flow through us and out to our neighbor."

If you're one of those church people who still draw color and class lines of human beings, it you're a member who is holding a grudge, it probably means that you desperately need to grow in your love of God and respect for your own self. Then you won't need to tramp on someone else in order to raise your opinion of yourself. It is only when we love God that many other people are loveable.

Charles L. Allen, in *God's Psychiatry*, tells about a scene from Amos and Andy. "There was a big man who would slap Andy across the chest whenever they met. Finally, Andy got enough of it and said to Amos, 'I'm fixed for him. I put a stick of dynamite in my vest pocket, and the next time he slaps me, he is going to get his hand blown off.' Andy had not reasoned that at the same time he would get his heart blown out." When we refuse to love our neighbor, we blow out our own heart. It all goes together. The brotherhood of people can become a reality only when we have the fatherhood of God.

This, then, becomes a test of our Christianity, of our worship and study and program as a congregation. Are we loving God? By being here, has our respect for ourselves deepened? Does all we do as a church and all you do as a Christian show your love of God and God's love for others?

The psychologist, Ferenizi, recently wrote what he thought was the plight of many gripers and complainers, and cranks. "They want to love their neighbor, but they don't know how. Never having received love, they cannot give love. They have become hard and cold, relentless and loveless, in their attitude toward life. This attitude has further isolated them from others. Though they are in the crowd, they are not a part of the fellowship." Is there any greater challenge to the Christian faith than to bring the love of God to these so they might love others?

Here is the difference between player and spectator in the congregation, between disciple and griper among us. What a beautiful obituary if it could be said of us as a congregation and individuals, "They respected themselves, they loved their God, and they loved all of God's people."

At the entrance to the harbor at the Isle of Man there are two lights. One would think that the two signals would confuse the pilot. But the fact is, he has to keep them in line; as long as he keeps them in line, his ship is safe. It is the same with these commands of Jesus: love of self, the love of God, and love others. When we keep them in line, we remain safe and well in the channel of the Christian life.

Jesus answered, "You must love the Lord your God with all your heart, with all your soul, and with all your mind . . . you must love your fellow man as yourself." (Matthew 22:37 & 39)

66

Reformation Sunday
John 8:31-36

Being Set Free

. . . "If you obey my teaching you are really my disciples; you will know the truth, and the truth will make you free." (John 8:31-32)

Today's Gospel promises us freedom, if we will truly be disciples of Christ. In fact, Jesus promises that if we will learn, know, and follow the truth, we will be set free. Remember, however, first we must become disciples.

Jesus tells us that to be a real disciple is to accept what he says about how great God is and how terrible sin is, and what the real meaning of life is. When we do this, we are starting to take the role of discipleship. In order to be a disciple, we are told to remain in the word.

The Scripture puts it: . . . "If you obey my teaching . . ." In order for us to obey his teaching, we study his Scripture, we listen for his voice before we make our decisions. To be a disciple means to completely immerse ourselves in the word, so when we decide those issues of life, it becomes our second nature to do what Christ's disciple would do.

We must also continue to grow in our understanding of Jesus. If we are to be a disciple, we must keep on expanding our spiritual knowledge. That means to be free is to be a real disciple; to be a real disciple is to learn and study him and his Scripture. When we decide we now "know it all," that we have arrived as a Christian, then we have ended our discipleship. Being a disciple means keeping an open and inquiring mind. It is arrogant and presumptuous and certainly not good discipleship to stop our growth anywhere along our chronological progress in life. This study, this being continually open to growth and learning, will lead us to see the truth. Jesus said, "You will know the truth, and the truth will make you free." (John 8:32) And what a marvelous truth our studying and growing gives us! We learn that the true values are in our life. We get a handle on that to which we ought to commit our lives.

In Maxwell Anderson's *Winterset*, Act II, Mio says: "Will you tell me how a man's to live, and face life, if he can't believe that truth is like a fire and will burn through and be seen — though it takes all the years there are? While I stand up and have breath in my lungs — I shall be one flame of that fire; it's all the life I have."

It is a freeing thing to finally be able to discern that which is good and worth a sacrifice from that which is junk in our lives. When we get this knowledge, we are freed up and know how to commit ourselves and how to spend our lives on that which is worthwhile.

Loretta Lynn, the miner's daughter from Kentucky, the number one country music vocalist, sings, "I Wanna Be Free." The Israelites wanted to be free from Egypt. The Prodigal Son wanted to be free from his family, Simon the Zealot wanted to be free from political tyranny. People taking drugs want to be free. Those who turn off the church want to be free from its influence. And many of those in society want to be free of the demands of the society around them. God never created you and me to be free in the popular sense of the word. He didn't intend for us to live just for our own selfish whims. Life is not just one big picnic; nor is the world a gigantic playground. Not a playground, but a vineyard, and God wants you and me to work in that vineyard. Romans 6:19 lays it out: "At one time you surrendered yourselves entirely as slaves to impurity and wickedness, for wicked purposes. The same way you must now surrender yourselves entirely as slaves of righteousness, for holy purposes."

You may be wondering just what are we free from when we become a true Christian?

William Barclay, in his little *Daily Study Bible* on the Gospel of John, lists four things which can enslave us, and from which we are free: fear, self, other people, and sin.

What a magnificent life our Lord is promising us if we are willing to be his disciples and get this freedom. We can be free from fear. Once we are the Lord's disciples, we are no more alone. We now have Christ "with us." The Emmanuel of Christmas becomes our "real presence" here with us now. When you have that kind of presence with Christ, you are never alone! Fear can leave because Christ is here. Hebrews 13:6 puts it: "Let us be bold, then, and say, The Lord is my helper, I will not be afraid. What can man do to me?"

Paul said to Timothy, "God has not given us the spirit of fear." With Martin Luther, we can exclaim, "A mighty fortress is our God." We are free from fear!

We are also free from ourselves. It is often true that we are our own worst enemies. Many of us don't like ourselves and feel enslaved to be the person we presently are, with no hope of change. But when we become Christ's disciple, and he becomes a presence with us, and we are in him, we have the power and ability to be a new person — one we can like and respect and live with in freedom.

Paul lays it out, "When anyone is united to Christ, there is a new creation; the old order has gone, and the new order has already begun." (2 Corinthians 5:17)

A parable by Rabindranath Tagore, Nobel Prize poet, reads, "I have on my table a violin string. It is free to move in any direction I like. If I twist one end, it responds; it is free. But it is not free to sing. So I take it and fix it into my violin. I bind it, and, when it is bound, it is free for the first time to sing." When we are bound to Christ, we are like that string — free to sing.

We are free from self, free from fear, and we are free from other people.

So much of our lives can be aimed at pleasing

everyone — doing what others do and want — worrying about what other people say or don't say. When we are freed as one of Christ's disciples, we don't worry about what other people will think, and we concentrate on what God thinks.

Mark Twain tells a quaint story of the man who spent years in prison, only to walk out one morning when he discovered that the door had never been locked! We are often that way with our Christian discipleship. We come to worship, we receive forgiveness, and we leave with the same long face and guilt that we came in with. It is such glorious freedom to get out of that slavery and worry and concern about pleasing everyone and trying to keep up with everyone. God becomes much more important than the Joneses. There is a greater freedom, not only from fear, from self, and from others, but also from sin.

We often sin not because we want to, or try on purpose to sin, but because we just can't seem to help it. Our way of life — our habits and weaknesses, our shortcomings — has often enslaved us, and we have heavy guilt on our backs.

"Show me," said Seneca, "anyone who is not a slave. One is a slave to lust, and another to avarice, and a third to ambition; all alike to fear." (*Interpreter's Bible*, Vol. VIII)

"No one," as Goethe put it, "is more of a slave than he who thinks himself free without being so." (*Interpreter's Bible*, Vol. VIII)

"Where one has once passed through the meadows, others are apt to follow, till a path is beaten broad and bare and hard. And a deed once done, tends to repeat itself, to harden into a habit, and to grow in time almost automatic. The thing we are doing may distress and humiliate us, yet it carries us away like a swimmer helpless in the raging waters that toss him where it will." (*Interpreter's Bible*, Vol. VIII)

We try, but we cannot free ourselves. To become one

of the disciples is to free us from that terrible load of guilt — to lift off the weight and to be free of those sins. We can be freed to be the person that God intended us to be. Put this up on your billboard of life: "We can break the slavery of sin."

"Oh, that a man may arise in me, that the man I am may cease to be." (Anonymous)

That's the kind of prayer we disciples can have answered: freedom from self, sin, fear, and others.

Jesus goes on to say in our Gospel, ". . . I tell you the truth; everyone who sins is a slave of sin. A slave does not belong to the family always, but a son belongs there forever. If the son makes you free, then you will be really free." (John 8:34-36)

Jesus said to us that we must be disciples, and that that makes us free, and then he tells us that it is Christ himself who frees us. Christ says he frees us as we learn and grow. To gain discipleship over our own lives is to gain knowledge about God, is to gain a freedom.

Socrates had demanded, "How can you call a man free when his pleasures rule over him?"

Paul wrote his thanks to God in Romans 6:17-20 for freedom from the slavery of sin that Christ had given him.

You have said, as I have, when someone scolds us for what we are doing, "I can do with my life as I please." But we can't! The point is that sin does with our lives — sin grabs hold and enslaves and only Christ can free us to do as we please, which is really as he pleases. Hate, ruthlessness, selfishness, alcohol and drugs, smoking, lust — these are all traps in our lives. Habits, prejudices, ungodliness — these can completely enslave us. It is only Christ who can give us back our freedom.

I have stood at the edge of Niagara Falls a number of times. The sight is spectacular. Some birds once were swooping down to snatch a drink from the clean water. A man told me how he had seen birds carried over the brink. They had dipped down for a drink, and ice had formed on their wings. Then they had dipped for another, and another, and more and more ice formed on their little bodies. Another dip or two and they could not rise. Over the Falls they went. Sin is as deceptive as the sparkling water of Niagara's wintry rapids. Dip into it once too often, and we are not able to lay aside the weight which sin gives us by clinging so closely.

It isn't a matter of doing what we like with our lives — we soon lose the power to do it. We become a slave to our own self-indulgences, prejudices, and selfishness, and they master us. But Jesus can set us free!

The story is told of Diogenes, the Greek philosopher who was captured by pirates and later put up for sale on the slave block. Looking around, Diogenes saw a vacant looking young man, very richly dressed, who stood by. "Sell me to that man," he said. "He looks as if he needs a master." We will indeed all have a master of one kind or another, and the scripture today encourages us to accept Christ for that master.

It was Jesus' point here, that if we sin we are not free. In fact, we are slaves. The Scripture, the message of our Savior, talks of liberation. Paul puts it . . . "All men have sinned and are far away from God's saving presence. But by the free gift of God's grace, they are all put right with him through Christ Jesus, who sets them free." (Romans 3:23-24)

The Scripture promises liberation. It is the sense and realization of that which gave the New Testament its atmosphere. Thus, it is the happiest book in literature.

When at last the day of their emancipation was breaking, the slaves of Jamaica, who had climbed to the summits of the highest hills that they might miss no moment of it, no sooner saw the sun's rim rise above the horizon than they laughed, wept, and sang, and danced, and fell upon their knees in prayer. But all alike kept crying in a kind of dazed and happy ecstasy, "Free! Free! Free!" That is the New Testament note. These people are always exulting in their newfound, incredible liberty

— incredible, yet true. "Where the spirit of the Lord is, there is freedom." (2 Corinthians 3:17)

A few years ago when I was in Atlanta, Georgia, my wife and I drove to the Atlanta cemetery to see the tomb of the famous Martin Luther King, Jr. I was deeply impressed by the words across the top of that tomb: "Free at last, free at last, thank God Almighty, free at last!"

We are free from fear, free from self, free from others, and free from sin. It is Jesus Christ and his discipleship that sets us free.

. . . "If you obey my teaching, you are really my disciples; you will know the truth, and the truth will make you free." (John 8:31-32)

All Saints' Sunday
Matthew 5:1-12

When We Mourn

"Jesus saw the crowds and went up a hill, where he sat down. His disciples gathered around him, and he began to teach them . . ." (Matthew 5:1-2)

Did you ever wish you could have been in on the heart to heart talks that Jesus had with that little band of twelve? In our Gospel for this All Saints' Sunday, we have what are called "Beatitudes" from the Sermon on the Mount. Matthew has a habit of collecting together all the sayings of Jesus on a particular subject and putting them together in his Gospel. Most scholars agree that this sermon on the mount is Matthew's collection and distillation and summary of Jesus' consistent teaching to his disciples.

He taught them many things many different times, and today we read in this fifth chapter of Matthew a summary of that teaching.

Matthew gives us some clues as to how important these sayings are. He says, "Jesus saw the crowds and went up a hill, where he sat down." (Matthew 5:1a) Jewish rabbis did their most important and official teaching from a sitting position. Jesus talked to them while they walked, but when he sat down, it was very important. This, then, is his official teaching. Matthew also says, " . . . and he began to teach them." (5:2) King James puts it, "when he had opened his mouth . . ." In the Greek this meant it was of grave importance. It was usually put before a terribly serious saying. It was also used to indicate a person was pouring out his heart in what he was saying. It meant a heart to heart, intimate conversation. Also, when Matthew said, ". . . he began to teach them . . .," the Greek here meant a repeated and habitual thing.

So we have here something Jesus taught them many times — it is the summary and the essence and the core of all that Jesus taught the disciples. You can see the words of the Gospel today must be treated with a special reverence, because they are the concentrated memory of many hours of teaching and conversation between Jesus and his disciples.

Under the heading "True Happiness," *Today's English Version* translates these beautitudes like this:

"Happy are those who know they are spiritually poor; the Kingdom of heaven belongs to them!

"Happy are those who mourn; God will comfort them!

"Happy are those who are humble; they will receive what God has promised!

"Happy are those whose greatest desire is to do what God requires; God will satisfy them fully!

'Happy are those who are merciful to others; God will be merciful to them!

"Happy are the pure in heart; they will see God!

"Happy are those who work for peace; God will call them his children!

"Happy are those who are persecuted because they do what God requires; The Kingdom of heaven belongs to them!

"Happy are you when people insult you, and persecute you, and tell all kinds of evil lies against you because you are my followers."

(Matthew 5:3-11)

When Jesus first spoke these words, they were exclamations. "O the joy of the meek!" This is important to understand, because it means that these exclamations are for now. They were not some future bliss prophesied. William Barclay, in his *Daily Study Bible* says, "They are

congratulations on what it." So let's say it here — that
the bliss promised Christians is not only in the future,
but is what we can have now. These beatitudes say —
"what a joy it is being a Christian now!" "Oh, the sheer
joy of following Christ now!"

So you see, we have joy *now* as we follow Jesus, and
are spiritually poor, and mourn, and are meek, and do
what God requires, and are merciful to others; and have
pure hearts; and we work for peace; and if we are
persecuted, and people persecute us. That's a happy,
joy-filled existence. And it is a description by Jesus of
our discipleship.

Celebrate with me today the fact that when Jesus
talked to his disciples out of the depths of his heart, he
promised us a joy and happiness in our worldly
discipleship. We not only have a promise of life with him
beyond the grave in a future state of bliss, but a full and
joy-filled life with him here and now! "Happy are those
who . . ." or "Blessed is the person . . ."

For this All Saints' Day, let's look at the second of
these summaries of the Christian life: "Happy are those
who mourn; God will comfort them!" (Matthew 5:4)

I have no doubt that this promise originally meant
that the person who was sorry for his sins, and thus
knew his need for forgiveness, is happy. It also meant
that happy or blessed is the person who identifies with
the sorrows of the world.

"Blessed are they that voluntarily share their
neighbor's pain. They could side-step it: 'It is not my
business; I have enough troubles of my own.' They could
even pretend that sorrow does not exist. But they
expose themselves to the world's misery. Like Arnold
von Winkelried, Swiss hero of the Battle of Sempach,
they stand in the pass and gather all the spears into their
own breasts. They visit the home where death has come.
They enter into the hidden tumult of the criminal in jail.
They agonize over slums and become leaders in civic
righteousness. None is bound, except they are bound.

They are the compassionate of the earth, and their reward is to grow in compassion." (*Interpreter's Bible*, Vol VII, page 282.)

There is indeed a promised joy in identifying with others' hurts and hurting with the knowledge of our own sin. In addition to all this, let's take this passage very literally: "Happy are those who mourn; God will comfort them."

The Greek word here for "to mourn" is one for mourning the dead — like Jacob's mourning when he thought his son Joseph was dead, like the grief you and I feel when death takes one of our loved ones.

That's a fantastic joy, isn't it? I believe this. I believe that what the Arabs claim is true: "All sunshine does make a desert." There are certain experiences that only come through grief.

I often quote this poem in my funeral sermons:

I walked a mile with Pleasure;
She chattered all the way,
But left me none the wiser
For all she had to say.
I walked a mile with Sorrow,
And ne're a word said she,
But, oh, the things I learned from her
When Sorrow walked with me!

"Only such have joy and song: only they are in tune. Joy is not the opposite of pain, or in respite of pain, or despite pain: it is because of pain, and through pain. Joy is sorrow accepted in contrite love. The mourners thus enter life's secret; others are barred at the door." (*Interpreter's Bible*, Vol. VII, page 282.)

When we mourn, we can find out anew how many friends we have who love us. It happens over and over again: someone close dies, and then we experience an outpouring of love from family and friends we never dreamed was possible.

Maggie was our Sarah's Beagle pup. We all loved the dog very much. Eleven-year-old Sarah was especially close. Those two — dog and daughter — were inseparable. Then, one of those very cold nights, Maggie followed the girls to play in the snow and got out on the highway and was crushed. She was frozen when we found her along the side-ditch. For an hour, our family sat in the family room and consoled each other. I held my Sarah for a long time, as she cried. Finally, we made our way up to our bedrooms, and with a big hug I kissed her good-night. That night we all learned again the blessedness of mourning.

It is joy to be loved like that! We also learn, when we mourn, the kind and depth of comfort God will give if we allow him. I am amazed over and over again the way that God can step into a desperate situation, pick us up when we're knocked down, and put us on our feet again.

When everything is all right — we don't often get down to basics. We just live on top of life, and never realize its full significance. But, often to lose a loved one and to grieve is not only to rediscover our loving friends, but is also to rediscover God's power to comfort and heal. When sorrow comes, we must face the important issues of life. We are driven to the deep things of our existence.

The promise you and I share here today which Jesus gave us is this: when we mourn, we are comforted by our fellow Christians. We find out the strength and love that can come from our God. And, we learn again that those who die in the Christian faith, the baptized believers, are provided for beyond the grave. Psalms 116:15 has it: "Precious in the sight of the Lord is the death of his saints."

It's right that in All Saints' Day sermons, we concentrate on the joy of the living, because we know that those who die in the Lord are okay. They, too, have their joy in Christ. He has prepared a place for them. The assurance of the Scripture leaps alive again for us: "Blessed are the dead which die in the Lord from henceforth: yea, saith the Spirit, that they may rest from their labors. . . . he that believeth in me, though he were dead, yet shall he live; and whosoever liveth and believeth in me shall never die."

We gain a new strength and a new beauty in our very souls because of our experience in mourning. We have a promise that God will give us care from our brothers and sisters in the faith, and also comfort from God himself. In addition to that, we have a new joy because we are put in touch again with genuine life and strength to live it.

> God hath not promised
>   Skies always blue,
> Flower-strewn pathways
>   All our lives through.
> God hath not promised
>   Sun without rain,
> Joy without sorrow,
>   Peace without pain.
> But God hath promised
>   Strength for the day,
> Rest for the labor,
>   Light for the way,
> Grace for the trials
>   Help from above
> Unfailing sympathy
>   Undying love.
>
> *Annie Flint*

In Robert Louis Stevenson's story of a storm, he describes a ship caught off a rocky coast threatening death to all on board. When terror among the people was at its worst, one man, more daring than the rest, making the perilous passage to the pilot house, saw the pilot lashed to his post, with his hands on the wheel and turning the ship little by little into the open sea. When the pilot saw the ghastly white, terror-stricken face of the man, he smiled, and the man rushed to the deck below, shouting: "I have seen the face of the pilot, and he smiled. All is well." The sight of that pilot's smiling face averted panic and converted despair into hope. So it is that the sight of the face of Christ and the knowledge of the love of God gives us a peace and comfort and confidence as we go through the process of mourning.

Jesus was summarizing a grand truth when he sat down, opened his mouth, and began to teach: "Happy are those who mourn; God will comfort them!"

Twenty-sixth Sunday after Pentecost
Matthew 23:1-12

For Those in Church:
Joy and Service

Matthew 23:1-12 is a good check list for our practice of religion. So many sermons are appropriate for all those Christians who are not there in church to hear them. This Gospel story and these comments are written especially for those who come to church — those of us who consider ourselves the faithful. Jesus spoke these words to his disciples. They are about the pillars of the church in his day — the scribes and Pharisees.

Rather then spend our time today giving thunder to the scribes and Pharisees (as often happens), let us see how Jesus' words affect the practice of our religion.

Jesus says about those scribes and Pharisees: ". . . they preach, but do not practice. They bind heavy burdens, hard to bear, and lay them on men's shoulders; but they themselves will not move them with their finger." (Matthew 23:3-4)

Our practice of the faith should be a help and not a burden. The scribes and Pharisees had worked out a religion based on many rules and regulations. The Ten Commandments were at the heart of it. They extended those commandments to include 613 rules!

The Commandments were simply two principles: reverence and respect. Reverence was the first three commandments and included reverence for God, for his day, and for the parents that he gave us. Respect marks the last seven commandments; respect for life, possessions, personality, good name, and one's self. The principles were correct — reverence for God and respect for people. But, the scribes and Pharisees took these simple principles and made them a burden, a worry by making religion a thing of rules and regulations.

Far too many Christians exhibit the spirit of the Buddhists of Burma, who have a saying: "Life is divided into three parts. The first part is for pleasure, the second is for accumulation of money and goods; the third is for religion."

Now let's check on our own presentation and practice of our faith.

Does our Christianity lift up or drag down? Are people helped by our faith, or haunted by it? Is the gospel we tell and live a threat, or a promise? Does it make Christianity a joy, or a burden? Does it threaten, or forgive? Does it have a sour face, or a smile?

If our Christianity depresses us, scares us, worries us, haunts us, it probably is not true Christian religion. The religion that Jesus presented to the disciples was one of support and comfort, peace and love, forgiveness and joy.

"It is this that made the future of Christianity," said Matthew Arnold, "its gladness, not its sorrow ... its drawing from the spiritual world a source of joy so abundant that it ran over upon the material world and transfigured it."

In one of the Reformed churches in France, in the chancel back of the pulpit there are three panels. The first is for the law, and the inscription on it is "Thou shalt love the Lord thy God." (Matthew 22:37) The second is for the gospel and the inscription upon it is the great verse from John (3:16): "God so loved the world, that he gave his only begotten son, that whosoever believeth in him should not perish, but have everlasting life." The third panel is for the Psalms, and the verse written upon it is that from Psalms 118 (14): "The Lord is my strength and song, and is become my salvation." Notice that the third panel says that the Lord is not only my strength, but my *song*. We sometimes do not emphasize enough, in the way we practice our Christianity, the fact that God is our song. We need to sing the joy of being in Christ when we worship as we live our lives throughout the week.

Certainly how we conduct ourselves here at worship in this building puts up signs for others to see and evaluate what our religion is like. If we are to be audio-visuals of the faith when we worship, then there certainly should be some accepting, warm smiles, some hugs, warm handshakes, laughter, comforting, encouraging, loving, accepting attitudes reflected in this place while we are together.

A contemporary described the secret of Dwight L. Moody's ministry in this manner: "I saw at once. Moody was simply bubbling over with the glory of his message. He reveled in it. His joy was contagious. Men leaped out of darkness into light and lived the Christian life from that hour."

"I might have been a minister myself," Oliver Wendell Holmes once said, "for ought I know, if a certain clergyman had not looked and talked like an undertaker."

Certainly Jesus gives good advice here — if our practice of Christianity is merely the "thou shalt nots," we just don't have the full gospel, the entire faith at all. The positive content is what gets us through, equips us to face and deal with life day by day. Holding a grudge against a pastor, remembering some of his or her mistakes, keeping alive hurt feelings from the past within the congregation, hating other denominations, will never help us when life tumbles in upon us. Knowing all the commandments by memory and keeping the letter of the Old Testament law will not be helpful equipment for us when the rug is yanked out from under us, and we must face life alone.

Jesus says religion is not a burden, but a joy.

Another warning in this Gospel is: Beware of showing off in our practice of the faith. The religion of the Pharisees was one of ostentation. If religion is keeping rules, if you keep rules, if you keep all of them, then you can acquire an air of perfection. Jesus selected certain practices where the Pharisees were showing off. He says, ". . . for they make their phylacteries broad and their fringes long, and they love the place of honor at feasts and the best seats in the synagogues, and salutations in the marketplaces . . ." (Matthew 23:5-7)

This business of phylacteries came from Exodus 13:9. The Jew wore it when he prayed. It was a little leather box strapped on the wrist or forehead — Scripture was written on a scroll inside the box. The Pharisee, in order to draw attention to himself, not only wore them, but made his larger than the rest to demonstrate his piety.

The tassel custom came from Numbers 15:37-41 and Deuteronomy 22:12 where God told his people to make fringes on their clothing, so they would be reminded of the Commandments. The Pharisees made them very large — so other people would see how pious they were.

The Pharisees also liked the choice seats at meals and the front seats at synagogues. (The most honored seats in those days were in the front of the church!)

The whole plan and practice of religion by these Pharisees was to call attention to themselves. Jesus says that our cause is just the opposite. We practice our faith in such a way that we are blocked out and God is glorified.

"Most men," said Thomas Erskine of Linlathen, "are so possessed by themselves that they have no vacuum into which God's deep water may rise."

"One of the smallest packages we ever saw was a man wrapped up wholly in himself," suggests an unknown writer.

Our whole practice of discipleship, our religion, is done not to say to the world, as did the Pharisee, "Look how good I am;" but rather, "Look what a wonderful God I have!" Any religion which encourages pride and showing off and self-righteousness is not true Christianity! Jesus did not teach us that kind of Christianity.

Joseph Fort Newton, in a commentary on modern times, wrote, "When a man loses faith in God, he worships humanity; when faith in humanity fails, he worships science, as so many are trying to do today. When faith in science fails, man worships himself, and at the altar of his own idolatry, he receives a benediction of vanity. Hence the tedious egotism of our day, when men are self-centered and self-obsessed, unable to get themselves off their hands."

No doubt, all of this which Jesus condemns was started as an enthusiastic practice of the faith. Here is where it is so difficult, and we must be so very careful. There is a fine line between witnessing with enthusiasm and being so caught up with our Christ, so on fire with the good news, that we must share it, and a sort of pious, self-righteous kind of religion which calls attention to ourselves rather than to the heavenly father we are excited about.

Carlton Van Ornum tells this story. A large crowd of people gathered near an enclosure in the Franklin Park Zoo in Boston as a peacock slowly spread his great tail and displayed its stunning plummage. The great bird stood erect and noble and strutted regally. Just then an old, dun-colored duck waddled slowly from the pond and passed between the proud peacock and the admiring crowd. Enraged, the peacock drove the duck back to the water. In a moment, the beautiful bird had become ugly with fierce anger. The plain and awkward duck, having returned to its natural habitat, was no longer unbecoming. In the water it swam and dived gracefully, unaware that many eyes were watching. The people who had admired the peacock loved the duck. Each of us was reminded of the dangers of pride, and that happiness comes from just being ourselves.

So while the first part of this Gospel warns us about making religion a burden instead of a joy, the second part warns us about exhibiting that joy in such a fashion as to call attention to ourselves instead of our great God. Then comes the admonition: Don't make religion a burden, don't show off the faith, do be a servant. He had said it already in Matthew 18:4 and Matthew 20:26. Jesus says here, "He who is greatest among you shall be your servant; whoever exalts himself will be humbled, and whoever humbles himself will be exalted." (Matthew 23:12)

As the Christian judges things, not keeping the religious rules or showing off your piety, but serving your fellow humans is real greatness. The world may claim that greatness is in commanding others to do things for us, but we claim it is in serving other people. Instinctively the world has accepted these standards. The world will respect, admire, and even fear the person with power — but it will love the person who serves.

Ask yourself who is really great and loved by people: it is the pastor who works among his people, the doctor who will help the sick any time, the employer who will take an interest in his employees, the person you can go to for help and never make you feel a nuisance.

Christianity isn't in shouting to the world "what a great Christian I am," or judging others or condemning them in a self-righteous attitude; but it is in helping our fellow humans. That's what greatness really is.

William Barclay writes in his *Daily Study Bible*, "When that great modern saint Kagawa first came into contact with Christianity, he felt its fascination, until one day the cry burst from him: 'Oh, God, make me like Christ.' To be like Christ, he went to live in the slums, and when he himself was suffering from tuberculosis. Cecil Northcott in *Famous Life Decisions* tells what Kagawa did. He went to live in a six-by-six foot hut in a Tokyo slum. On his first night he was asked to share his bed with a man suffering from a contagious itch — he welcomed his bedfellow. Then a beggar asked for his shirt and got it. The next day he was back for Kagawa's coat and trousers and got them, too. The slum dwellers laughed at him, but they came to respect him. He stood in the driving rain to preach, coughing all the time. 'God is love,' he shouted. 'God is love. Where love is, there is God.' He often fell down exhausted, and rough men of the slums carried him gently back to his hut.

"Kagawa himself wrote, 'God dwells among the lowliest of men. He sits on the dustheap among the prison convicts. He stands with the juvenile delinquents. He is there with the beggars. He is among the sick, he stands with the unemployed. Therefore, let him who would meet God visit a prison cell before going to the temple. Before he goes to church, let him visit the hospital. Before he reads the Bible, let him help the beggar.'"

Therein lies greatness. The world may judge a person's greatness by his bank account, or the people he controls, or his academic credentials, or the material possessions he has gathered. But, Jesus asks, "How many people have you helped?"

If we want to practice genuine Christianity, we will serve our fellow humans, not show off our religion, and present the faith as a joy and not a burden.

Twenty-seventh Sunday after Pentecost
Matthew 24:1-14

While We Watch for the Coming

The twenty-fourth chapter of Matthew is a tough one! Some preachers are not honest with its interpretation. In this chapter the author of Matthew gathers together interweaving strands of material about the future. The sentences are all mixed up, and they deal with six different subjects of the future. There is advice given by Jesus as to what to expect.

1. The attack in Jerusalem by Titus. "So when you see the desolating sacrilege spoken of by the prophet Daniel, standing in the holy place, . . . then let those who are in Judea flee to the mountains." (Matthew 24:15,16)

2. The destruction of Jerusalem. Verses 1 and 2 ". . . Truly, I say to you, there will not be left here one stone upon another." (Matthew 24:2)

3. The Jewish idea of "the day of the Lord." Verses 6 -8. **"And you will hear of wars and rumors of wars; see** that you are not alarmed; for this must take place, but the end is not yet." (Matthew 24:6)

4. Persecution of the followers of Christ. Verses 9 and 10. "Then they will deliver you up to tribulation, and put you to death." (Verse 9)

5. Threats against the Christian church. Verses 4 and 5, 11-13. ". . . Take heed that no one leads you astray." (Matthew 24:4b)

6. Then there are the verses referring to the second coming of Christ. Verses 3 and 14: "And this gospel of the kingdom will be preached throughout the whole world, as a testimony to all nations; and then the end will come." (Matthew 24:14)

That bunch of Galilean fishermen didn't get to the big

city of Jerusalem very often, and this time when they did, they expressed their awe and wonder at the temple area — that majestic white marble with gold that shone in the sun. We read Jesus' answer in verse two — the *Today's English Version* puts it: ". . . You may well look at all these. I tell you this; not a single stone here will be left in its place; every one of them will be thrown down." (Matthew 24:2)

Jesus says the Holy City will fall. I suppose that was shocking news to these disciples. This, the Holy City, the dwelling place of God, this location of the pious priests and clergy was doomed. Jesus was correct. In A.D. 70 the Romans got fed up and exasperated by the rebellious Jews — gave up, and tore the temple and city to bits. Jesus' prophecy literally came true.

So here is Jesus playing the role of a prophet. There wasn't any magic in his knowledge. Jesus was saying that if the Jews continued to play the game of power politics, it would end in their own downfall. The nation and people who will not take God and his will into their strategy are bound to fall — they are heading for disaster even in material things. William Barclay puts it, "The man and the nation, which refuse the dream of God, will find their own dreams shattered also."

Harry K. Zeller, Jr., writes: "The featured speaker at a local meeting celebrating American Education Week spoke with keen and incisive language on the kind of education the world needs today. He pointed out that our schools tend to lift our national aspirations above those of other people and to glorify the flag with a degree of reverence. 'But,' he added, 'the atomic and hydrogen bombs often offer possibilities for universal destruction, and in the future, we shall have to think of our nation as an equal unit with other nations in a world family and our flag on a par with other flags of the nations of the world. We must begin to teach these concepts in the schools of the nation, or we will perish.' There was a general agreement with the logic of his thought. 'But —,' he paused long and ominously, 'if ever the school authorities attempted to teach this in your city, you men who have today elected school leaders would be the first to join every patriotic civic group in the community and bend every effort to drive these leaders out of town!'"

The country that fails to take God into its strategy and concern is bound to fall, says Jesus. In the United States Senate, Peter Marshall prayed: "Help us, our Father, to show other nations an America to imitate — not the America of loud jazz music, self-seeking indulgence, and love of money, but the America that loves fair play, honest dealing, straight talk, real freedom, and faith in God. Make us to see that it cannot be done as long as we are content to be coupon-clippers from the original investment made by our forefathers. Give us faith in God and love for our fellow men, that we may have something to deposit on which the young people today can draw interest tomorrow." (*The Congressional Record*, Washington)

About the persecution of his followers Jesus said, "Then you will be arrested and handed over to be punished and be put to death. All mankind will hate you because of me." (Matthew 24:9)

It's always true, if we are the real church, we will always be persecuted, because we live in a world that is sinful and not a Christian world. Notice Jesus doesn't promise that it would be easy if you become one of his disciples — he never promised an easy way, but rather the stuff to endure and get through.

In a letter to his friend Donatus, Cyprian, Bishop of the Church at Carthage in the third century, wrote: "This is a cheerful world, as I see it from my garden under the shadows of my vines. But if I were to ascend some high mountain and look out over the wide lands, you know well what I should see: brigands on the highways, pirates on the sea, armies fighting, cities burning, in the amphitheatres men murdered to please applauding crowds, selfishness and cruelty and misery and dispair under all roofs. It is a bad world, Donatus, an incredibly bad world. But I have discovered in the midst of it a quiet and holy people who have learned a great secret. They have found a joy that is a thousand times better than any pleasure of our sinful life. They are despised and persecuted, but they care not. They are masters of their souls. They have overcome the world. These people, Donatus, are the Christians — and I am one of them."

Why is it that if we are Christian, we will be persecuted? A number of reasons come to mind.

We Christians set an example of a beautiful life, and that makes other lives look ugly by comparison. It's an example to the rest of the world that makes people uncomfortable. We demonstrate the Christ-filled life, and those who live the Christ-less life are angry and jealous.

Christianity calls for change in our life, and many do not want to change. We march by a different drummer, and the way we live life in Christ calls to task the standards of others in their life-style, in their personal relationships, and their business ethics.

We demand Jesus Christ have first place in our lives — and that will cause many clashes with those who don't. Our priorities and loyalties are different. These surpass all earthly loyalties.

We, if we are Christ's disciples, are a conscience in life. We must not hide our desire for what is right over wrong. We are the conscience of our community, and there are always those who would like to silence conscience.

So it is true, if we practice discipleship, we'll encounter persecution. If we haven't experienced it, perhaps we are falling short of the mark of being Christ's people.

Howard W. Smith writes, "When the Roman

Emperor threatened to banish Chrysostom, the early Christian preacher, he answered: Thou canst not, for the world is my father's house. Thou canst not banish me.' When the emperor threatened to kill him, he said, 'Thou canst not, for my life is hid with Christ in God.' When he threatened to take away his treasure, Chrysostom said: 'My treasure is in heaven, and my heart is there.' Finally the emperor said he would take away his friends. To this the Christian said: 'That thou canst not, for I have a friend in heaven from whom thou canst not separate me. I defy thee; there is nothing thou canst do to hurt me.'"

"They may kill me if they please," said Savonarola, "but they will never, never, never tear the living Christ from my heart!"

Threats against the faith are also indicated as something that will happen to us while we wait for the second coming of Christ. In verses four, five, and eleven to thirteen of this text, we read about them. Jesus answered, "Watch out, and do not let anyone fool you. Because many men will come in my name, saying, 'I am the Messiah!' and fool many people." (Matthew 24:4-5)

Jesus warns us against false leaders. That's always one of the dangers facing the church. There are always those who use Christianity to promote themselves and build their own little kingdom, rather than God's kingdom. There are always those who teach their own version of the truth — spread their own ideas — claim they have a monopoly on God's grace. Jesus says beware of those who claim to be the Messiah — who point to themselves rather than to God.

The real test is to ask, "Is that person like Christ?" The effect of these false leaders is eventual dissension in the church and bigots as its membership.

Roy L. Smith tells in *The Christian Advocate*, "We have heard of a community that has been crying for leadership for the past five years, but when a leader appeared the other day, they crucified him."

Charles L. Wallis said, "It is reported that Colonel Theodore Roosevelt at San Juan Hill never said 'Go!' to his Roughriders. Always his command was, 'Come on, boys.'"

Laurence of Arabia, one of the most colorful characters in World War I wrote of the Arabs: "No man could be their leader except he ate the rank's food and wore their clothes, lived on a level with them, and yet appeared better in himself."

That's real, and not false, leadership. Jesus saw false leaders as a threat to his church, and he also saw discouragement as a danger. But if we are disciples, we don't give up, no matter how hopeless the world seems. God is not dead; he is not absent; we need not be discouraged; we shall overcome.

The devil, according to legend, once advertised his tools for sale at public auction. When the prospective buyers assembled, there was one oddly-shaped tool which was labeled "Not for Sale." Asked to explain why this was, the devil answered, "I can spare my other tools, But I cannot spare this one. It is the most useful implement that I have. It is called *Discouragement*, and with it I can work my way into hearts otherwise inaccessible. When I get this tool into a person's heart, the way is open to plant anything there I may desire." The legend embodies sober truth. Discouragement is a dangerous state of mind because it leaves one open to the assault of the enemies of the soul.

Napoleon used to say of his famous marshall, Massena, that he had a remarkable reserve strength, and that he was never himself until the tide of battle began to turn against him. He took new life from what to many would bring discouragement.

Discouragement can be devastating in a congregation among Christians. It is always a threat there. We are prone to say, "We've tried that before," or "We're not large enough to do that," or "We're not strong enough," or "We don't have the resources." You know all the discouraged put-downs that can sneak into our strategy and weaken our witness in the community. Jesus said to beware of these dangers and false leaders and discouragement.

Jesus also speaks here of the "second coming." The New Testament doesn't even use this word — the word it uses is "parousia" — this chapter is the only place it appears in the Gospels. It describes a king coming to his subjects. Here he says, "And this Good News about the Kingdom will be preached throughout all the world, for a witness to all mankind; and then will come the end." (Matthew 24:14)

There are a lot of ideas about the Parousia, the Second Coming; whatever else you believe, it does announce two great ideas: one, the ultimate triumph of Jesus Christ. Even though we crucified him, one day he will win out. For Christ the end is sure — and the end is the kingship of the world.

Two, let's sing it out: History is going somewhere. Some have felt that history is simply a record of our mistakes. Some have felt that it is a vicious circle in which we repeat our miseries. That's an awful view of things — that we are on an endless treadmill in which we make no progress and from which we cannot escape. But the Second Coming of Christ has a great truth in it. It is not all futile and hopeless. We are moving toward a great event. That event is not a catastrophe, but rather the eternal rule of God.

Clarence E. Macartney says: "In Sherman's march from Chattanooga to Atlanta, and from Atlanta to the sea, the Confederate government, impatient with the Fabian tactics of General Johnston, removed him from command and gave his army to the impetuous General

Hood. Hood at once marched to the rear of Sherman, threatening his communications and base of supplies at Chattanooga and Nashville. An important link to these communications was Allatoona, which commanded the pass through the mountains. This post was at once attacked by Hood's army. Sherman sent an order to one of his lieutenants, Corse, to proceed to Allatoona. He, himself, went back as far as Kenesaw Mountain, and from that experience on the clear October day, could see plainly the smoke of the battle and hear the faint reverberation of the cannon. His flag officer at length made out the letters which were wigwagged from the garrison at Allatoona. 'Corse is here.' This was a great relief to Sherman, who then heliographed his famous message, 'Hold the fort. I am coming.'"

That incident inspired a gospel hymn "Hold the Fort, for I Am Coming!" The inspired hymn has genuine truth in its lines. The Christian is to occupy until Christ comes. Christ has not left us without a promise, which means deliverance and victory. From the ramparts of heaven he waves to us the message that he is coming.

These passages of scripture touch on many things, but mainly it wants to tell us what to expect and how to behave while we wait for the coming of Christ:

— We must beware of false leaders and discouragement;
— Followers of Jesus will be persecuted;
— Cities will fall without Christian faith and influence;
— We can look forward to the second coming of Christ.

Christ the King
The Last Sunday after Pentecost
Matthew 25:31-46

Christ the King

The king of an African tribe, after many years, faced the fact that his throne was wearing out. It was repaired a couple of times, but eventually collapsed and was replaced with a new one. The king, for sentimental reasons, hated to part with his old throne. So it was hoisted on ropes to the ceiling of his grass hut and stored there. Then one night during a storm, the throne fell down and hit the king on the head. The moral of the story is that people who live in grass houses shouldn't stow thrones.

We talk about kings and kingdoms today.

I traveled to Izmir, Turkey, not long ago, and there I remembered again the town Smyrna mentioned by John in the Book of Revelation. I saw St. Polycarp's church and recalled Harry Emerson Fosdick's tale: In A.D. 156, Polycarp, a Christian martyr, was put to death in Smyrna and the small struggling Christian community was terrified by the persecution under the proconsulship of Statius Quadratus, and was heartbroken by its leader's death. The man who wrote the record of it, however, for the centuries to read, boiled down a great truth into a few words when he dated the event. 'Statius Quadratus, proconsul,' he wrote, 'Jesus Christ, King forever.'" Fosdick goes ahead to say that he wonders if that person guessed that in the Twentieth Century we should be reading that. Who was "Statius Quadratus, proconsul?" Long since sunk into oblivion! But still above the world's turmoil the affirmation resounds, "Jesus Christ, King forever."

Today is one of the newer church observances. The last Sunday after Pentecost, before we launch into the new church year and Advent, on this last Sunday of the church year, we celebrate Christ the King.

There is something grand and glorious about the festival. We spend a lot of time talking about Jesus as meek and humble through the church year, but today unashamed we see our Savior as a king.

Jesus said, "When the Son of Man comes in his glory, and all the angels with him, then he will sit on his glorious throne." (Matthew 25:31)

The New Testament is full of the analogy of kings and kingdoms and yet, that isn't very relevant to us in the United States who have never known anything except a congress and an elected president.

However, those who were around Jesus didn't seem to understand his claims of kingdoms and kingship then either. They thought he meant a political king who would drive the Romans out of Jerusalem. When he fed the crowds, the Scripture says that they wanted to make him king. He explained over and over again with his parables what his kingdom was really like.

Richard Roberts tells of a student of Tolstoy who was hauled into court for refusing military service. When he defended himself by quoting from the Gospels, the judge impatiently said, "But that is the Kingdom of Heaven; and it has not yet come." The student replied, "Sir, it may not have come for you, but is has for me." Today's Scripture tells us about the King and his Kingdom and how they come to us.

The Gospel from Matthew begins by telling of the King on his throne separating sheep and goats, and then we have the words, "Then the King will say to those at his right hand, 'Come, O blessed of my Father, inherit the kingdom prepared for you from the foundation of the world; for I was hungry and you gave me food, I was thirsty and you gave me drink, I was a stranger and you welcomed me, I was sick and you visited me, I was in prison and you came to me.'" (Matthew 25:34-36)

There is a bold and frightening lesson in this parable: God will judge us by seeing how we react to human need. God's judgment does not depend on how much we learn, or how popular we are, or how regular we are in our church attendance, or how much money we have saved, but on how much help we have given to those who need it.

We have the promise here that it is help which we give to others and which we don't even realize or calculate. Notice that in this story, they hadn't realized that they had helped. ". . . Lord, when did we see thee hungry and feed thee . . ." When we have Jesus Christ as our King, and he is on the throne of our earthly lives, we will make automatic responses to others' needs. For subjects of Christ the King, it is the natural thing to do. In Book I of *The Harbor*, Ernest Poole writes: "Though (my mother) was a strong church woman, I heard little from her of the terrors of hell. But I heard much of heaven, and more still of a heaven on earth. 'Thy will be done on earth, as it is in heaven.' I can never forget how she spoke those words as I knelt and repeated them after her — not so much in the tone of a prayer to a higher being, as in one of quiet resolve to herself. To do her share, through church and hospitals and charity work and the bringing up of her children, her share in the establishment of a heaven upon earth, this was her religion."

Out of an overflow of our hearts we just must help. With no thought of reward or merit or "brownie points" with anyone, we want to do the deed. In concert with the heart of our king, we respond; instinctively we help.

Be sure, all of religion is not in giving a buck to a beggar or doing some charity. But such charity coming out of love of Christ is an essential act, without which faith dries up and dies.

It is a beautiful thing when you and I have a heart that can be touched and that is sensitive and compassionate. If you are one who brags about being "self-made" and "shrewd" and never being taken advantage of, you may have the wrong king on the throne. Often our little bit of response is for the wrong reason. It can be selfish motivation that moves us to help and thus receive the praise and thanks. We have manipulated our own ego trip. That isn't the way it is for those in Christ the King's kingdom. We're tender-hearted subjects who must respond to needs of people. That means all sorts of people who need us.

There is something else here. Notice we aren't asked to do the grand, dramatic thing, but rather the little everyday help. A cup of water, or something to eat, some clothing, visitation of the ill, going to see someone in prison — these are the deeds that count in the kingdom of Christ. Jesus, in telling this parable, wanted us to know that the little spontaneous, loving gestures are the ones that are significant. We so often make the mistake of thinking in terms of gifts of a thousand dollars or large endowments or the spectacular work or contribution: Those surely help in the kingdom, but we must always look for the opportunity to respond to the simple, human help of the people we meet each day.

"The criterion of judgment is a daybreak and astonishment. From the sea of faces each person is singled out in turn. He is asked not about his creed or his worship or his standing in the community, but, 'What have you done for the family on the other side of town? Ever make any visit to the local jail?' The hungry, the thirsty, the homeless, the naked, the physically afflicted, and the prisoner are made the test. What we have done for them, or failed to do, is judgment on us by our king. Notice well the list; such people require of us sympathy, both in imagination and in the deed. They demand real self-denial, for none of the unfortunates mentioned can quickly make recompense. They ask obedience to God's quickening within us, for 'love is of God.'" (1 John 4:7 — *The Interpreter's Bible*, Vol. XII)

This story surely does give us "little folks" an important opportunity to serve the King — the lonely who need someone to talk with on the visitation team, the cold who need a few pieces of clothing in Church World Relief, the extra offering requested for the Salvation Army, the transcient who needs a pair of shoes, the Ohio State Reformatory resident who needs a letter, the refugee who needs a new start in a new country. If Christ is our King and on the throne, and we are really his subjects, we will respond instinctively with those little gestures that mean so much.

Another thing we learn about our King is: "And the King will answer them, 'Truly, I say to you, as you did it to one of the least of these my brethren, you did it to me.'" (Matthew 25:40) That's a real surprise, isn't it? That our King says that when we help someone, we are helping him; and when we refuse to help, we are refusing none less than the King! Consider again, with this additional information, your saying a hard "no" to the last appeal that your church made to you for help and support. It seems odd. Yet, it is so, isn't it? If you give something to my son, you have given to me. If you refuse my children, you have refused me. Our God is the Father, and when we help his children, we help him. His children are our fellow persons.

William Barclay in his *Daily Study Bible* on Matthew tells of two men who found this parable "blessedly true." "The one was Francis of Assissi; he was rich and wealthy and he was high-born and he was high-spirited, but he was not happy. He felt that life was incomplete. Then one day he was riding, and he met a leper, loathsome and repulsive in the ugliness of his disease. Something moved Francis to dismount and fling his arms around this wretched sufferer; and, lo, in his arms the face of the leper changed to the face of the Christ.

"The other was Martin of Tours. He was a Roman soldier, and a Christian. One cold winter day, as he was entering a city, a beggar asked him for alms Martin had no money, but the beggar was blue and shivering with cold, and Martin gave what he had. He took off his soldier's coat, worn and frayed as it was; he cut it in two and gave half of it to the beggarman. That night he had a dream. In it he saw the heavenly places and all the angels and Jesus in the midst of them; and Jesus was wearing one-half of a Roman soldier's cloak. One of the angels said to Him, 'Master, why are you wearing the battered old cloak? Who gave it to you?' Jesus answered softly, 'My servant Martin gave it to me.'"

Christ is indeed king, but like some fabled ruler, he walks through the streets in beggar's clothing.

There is a joy in giving the simplest things to people who need, because we soon have the joy of helping our King. What a glorious picture Jesus gives to us. He tells us to respond if we are really his subjects, and he is our King. He tells us we indeed do have a king, that God rules, he is in control. He is on the throne and we need not be afraid. And the promise is . . . "but the righteous into eternal life." (Matthew 25:46).

So we have from our King a promise of eternal life. A life not so much by duration, but rather, by quality. It is a new, rewarding fulfilling life in the kingdom of our King.

When we help the unfortunate, we help Christ. It is often the simplest things that our King asks us to do for others. We are judged by the help we give to our fellow persons. Christ is indeed on the throne and our King.

One Palm Sunday in the city of Florence, 450 years ago, Savonarola was preaching to a great multitude. Suddenly, in the middle of his discourse he cried aloud: "It is the Lord's will to give a new head to this city of Florence." For a moment he paused, keeping the people in suspense, and then he went on: "The new head is Christ! Christ seeks to become your King." And with that the whole multitude were on their feet, shouting: "Long live Jesus, King of Florence!"